Praise for *You Don't Owe Anyone*

"I could not stop reading this book; I felt seen in ways no book has ever made me feel. Caroline is a masterful storyteller, and her honesty is so comforting. This is a magnificently brave work, one that offers fellow pleasers and strivers an invitation to claim healthier and happier ways of being in the world."

—Rachel Macy Stafford, *New York Times* bestselling author, speaker, and certified special education teacher

"So often we give ourselves away in the search for acceptance. *You Don't Owe Anyone* is a much-needed reminder that this sense of belonging is really only found when we look inward. But for some of us, this introspection can be truly harrowing. I know what it's like to not feel safe in your own skin. This book guides you to create that safe, loving space in yourself. For those who have struggled to trust themselves, this book is a true companion."

—Julie Barton, *New York Times* bestselling author of *Dog Medicine*

"Reading this book is like having a heart-to-heart with a wise, dear friend who reminds you how to come back home to yourself. Caroline is an expert at unlocking old trauma patterns so you can break free and shine your light."

—Elisa Boxer, author and Emmy Award–winning journalist

"Caroline's book is packed with practical wisdom, delivered in the encouraging voice of a big sister who's rooting for you to move out of the 'try-hard' cycle of perfectionism and onto the path of your own unique journey. This book gives us permission to make our inner freedom (which is not an indulgence) our number-one priority—a message that is greatly needed in this time."

—Kelly McNelis, founder of Women for One, and author of *Your Messy Brilliance: 7 Tools for the Perfectly Imperfect Woman*

"As soon as I heard the title, I knew I had to read this book. When I did, I was swept along with each story. This is brilliant, strong work; it's the permission slip every perfectionist needs to clutch to their heart."

— Deborah Hurwitz, founder and CEO of COBALT Coaching

"Whether you're a people pleaser or a perfectionist, overcommitted or overwhelmed, you'll find sweet relief in these pages. Through personal stories and practical advice, Caroline shows you how to give yourself more care, kindness, and grace."

—Francine Jay, author of *The Joy of Less* and *Lightly*

"I want to thrash around wildly and cry and scream and yell and then shove this book into the hands of every single person I've ever met and say, 'Here, you *have* to read this.' For the people pleasing, always-there-for-everyone, never-let-a-ball-drop overextenders, overworkers, and overachievers: this book will make you burn it all down . . . and rejoice. It's the perfect book for perfectionists. Ironic? Maybe. Imperative? Definitely."

—Ash Ambirge, Author, Entrepreneur, CEO

You Don't Owe Anyone

Free Yourself from the Weight of Expectations

Caroline Garnet McGraw

Broadleaf Books
Minneapolis

To Tam, for keeping the faith,
to Brooke, for helping me hope,
to Jonathan, for being my love.

Contents

Introduction

What If You Didn't Owe Anyone?

HAVE YOU EVER BEAT yourself up over not responding to every message you received in a day?

Me too. I know how it goes. On one hand, you're tired and overwhelmed. But on the other hand, there are emails! Texts! Calls! All demanding a response!

If we check in with ourselves, we can sense which messages require our attention. However, we have trouble heeding that inner knowing because it conflicts with what we've been taught:

/ If someone writes, we must write back.
/ If someone starts talking, we must converse.
/ If someone moves in for a hug, we must embrace.

It doesn't matter if we feel uncomfortable, exhausted, or just plain unwilling. If we don't do these things, then we're unkind and rude. Right?

Maybe not.

Maybe there are more important questions for us to ask ourselves than, "But what if they get mad at me?"

Questions such as,

/ How much time have I wasted in needing to be seen a certain way?
/ What danger have I courted with my inability to say a direct no?
/ What have I sacrificed on the altar of being too nice?

It isn't easy to answer these questions, I know. But years ago, I came face-to-face with them.

A male acquaintance who had made a drunken move on me a decade prior—and whom I hadn't spoken to since—sent me a series of messages on Facebook. There was no context to the messages, just "I miss you." "I miss you." "I really miss you."

Perhaps it's obvious to you that these messages did not require a response. But at the time, it wasn't clear to me. (Have you ever noticed that other people's problems seem simple to solve, whereas our own struggles feel much more complex?)

For me, the thought of not responding triggered feelings of guilt and insecurity. What if I hurt this guy's feelings? Was I not being compassionate enough? Should I be polite or listen to my intuition?

Eventually, I asked my husband, Jonathan, for his perspective. "You don't owe anyone an interaction," he said fiercely.

When Jonathan said those six words, something within me unlocked. For three decades I'd been held captive by my own mistaken beliefs, but in that moment, I understood that I could set myself free. Suddenly, it was obvious: I did not have to respond to the messages at all. I did not have to twist myself into knots just because a man said that he missed me. I did not have to protect him from his discomfort while ignoring my own. It was OK for him to miss me, but it wasn't OK for me to miss myself anymore. I did not owe him—or anyone else—an interaction. There was no debt to pay.

All I could say in response to Jonathan was "Wow. May I quote you on that?"

He said yes, so I published a post expanding on his core idea. I wrote about how many women feel compelled to respond to everyone who reaches out to them. I wrote about how we've been conditioned to believe that being kind means being available 24/7, but when we don't guard our time, our very ability to be kind erodes.

The topic touched a nerve. "You Don't Owe Anyone an Interaction" went viral on the *Huffington Post* and led to my subsequent TEDx talk, which was quoted in the *Harvard Business Review*. Clearly, this is a collective struggle.

WHERE DID IT BEGIN for you, dear one? When did you start believing that you owed the whole world? When did you shoulder the burden of being "good" and start keeping your real self hidden away? And when did you realize that it wasn't working, that it was taking you to a place you never wanted to go?

Those of us who strive for perfection yet feel surrounded by shame can trace these patterns back to our early lives. We remember pivotal moments, times when we made crucial decisions about our place in the world.

One of my big moments came at age five. That was the year that I went with my mom and three-year-old brother Willie to a diagnostic center. Mom and Willie went into an office while I played on the jungle gyms in the waiting area. The sunlight streamed through the windows, and it all seemed very peaceful.

By the time our mother came back through the doors, though, everything had changed. She knelt down to hold me tightly, almost desperately. There were tears on her face, tears running into her hair. I didn't understand why she was sad. But I did understand that my mother needed *me* to comfort *her*.

I found out later that the diagnostic center was called Eden Autism Services and that "Pervasive Developmental Disorder, Not Otherwise Specified" was the reason why Willie wouldn't look me in the eye. And while I didn't know anything about autism, I did know that Willie loved me because he'd sit next to me when we watched TV and let me cuddle him longer than anyone else.

In 1990, there was little in the way of autism awareness; our family was in uncharted territory. After the day at the diagnostic center, our parents sat me down and told me that there was something different about Willie's mind, that he did things in his own way. They reassured me that I didn't need to worry because he would be OK and we would be OK. But I would need to be patient and kind, a good daughter, a good older sister.

Could I do that? they asked me. Could I be good?

"Yes," I said. "Yes, I will be good."

Those words were my solemn vow. Frankly, it was a relief to speak them aloud. I appreciated having a clear role, a purposeful way to help our family. Willie would be different, and I would be good, and we would all be OK. It became a simplistic equation in my psyche: one different boy plus one good girl equals a family in which everyone is OK. From that point forward, being "good" was my safe place. Sure, it was hard work, but at least it gave me a sense of control. It seemed like a small price to pay.

───

DO YOU KNOW WHAT it's like to hide your true self behind perfectionism and a keep-it-all-together facade? To try so hard not to disappoint others, to take on the "good girl" or "good boy" as your primary identity?

If so, then you know that this kind of behavior brings some big rewards. When you learn to overfunction and act like an adult from an early age, actual adults give you more and more responsibility. You receive awards and accolades, praise and promotions. People tell you that you're their shining star, and you smile and nod and pretend that your herculean workload is easy. Sure, no problem! It's all under control!

Or maybe you prefer to fly under the radar, to hide in a different way. Maybe your form of escape isn't perfectionism but people-pleasing. Maybe a long time ago you decided that the way to be safe was to be everyone's best friend, to be the person they could always count on to help. So now you say yes when you mean no, over and over again.

Either way, there's a disconnect. You show up one way—strong, brave, kind, or helpful—when your deeper truth is something different. Something messier and much less acceptable.

But before we continue, there's something that you should know about this book.

I understand that when you pick up a personal development book, you're probably looking for meaning in your struggle and answers to your own issues.

And though of course I'm here to help you have what you want, this book doesn't take the usual approach.

I'm not going to give you lists of how-tos and life hacks. I'm not going to tell you that this is the best or the only approach to personal growth. It's just one signpost on the lifelong walk toward wholeness. So if there's anything in these pages that doesn't resonate with your own deep sense of truth, then please let it go. Keep only what serves you. You are the expert on you!

Instead of giving you answers, I'm going to give you something better. I'm going to give you stories.

It's a more personal approach because, frankly, that's what has helped me the most on my own journey. The books I treasure and reread aren't the ones with lots of bullet-point lists. Rather, they're the ones where the authors risked telling real stories. Fiction or non-fiction, it doesn't matter—you can tell when an author is letting you into the truth of our shared humanity. You can feel it.

One such author, Philip Pullman, said it well:

"We don't need a list of rights and wrongs, tables of dos and don'ts: we need books, time, and silence. Thou shalt not is soon forgotten, but Once upon a time lasts forever."

Though the stories I share here are nonfiction, this is a "once upon a time" sort of book.

So here's where we begin. Once upon a time, I trusted a stranger more than myself.

Have you ever done that—ever gone with what an authority figure told you that you should do even though deep down you knew better? And have you ever had that decision put you in danger?

———

HERE'S WHAT I NEVER knew about car crashes before I was in one: when an airbag deploys, it releases dusty, chemical-scented clouds into the air. Those clouds were the first thing I saw when I opened my eyes after the accident, and they made the interior of the Chrysler Concorde look so strange and otherworldly that for a split second I thought that I was dead.

Once I realized that the mistiness around me came from the air-bags and not the clouds of heaven, I knew that I'd made a massive mistake. The accident was all my fault.

Why, oh why did I make that stupid blind turn? I wondered. *Why did I value that stranger's hand waving me forward over my own hesitation? Why do I trust other people more than I trust myself?*

A high-school junior at the time, I was a high achiever, deeply invested in never making mistakes. But this was a big one. En route to school, I'd been preparing to make a left turn at a green light. When the large SUV coming the opposite way blocked my view of oncoming traffic, I'd paused, but the other driver had waved me forward with confidence. As I'd overrode my hesitation and turned the steering wheel, a minivan with the right of way drove through the intersection at full speed.

Why did I make that stupid blind turn? It was an important question. But it wasn't really the time to ponder, since I sat in a crunched-up car in the middle of a busy street. As soon as I could get my shaky legs to cooperate, I released the seat belt and launched myself out the door.

The car was totaled, but I had no visible injuries, so I made my way over to the side of the road in front of a Catholic church. When I saw that the minivan I'd hit was a transport van for adults with special medical needs, though, my knees buckled. I crumpled to the curb and cried. The sight of the adults' frightened faces was too much. Ashamed, I couldn't even look at the vulnerable men and women. Though thankfully they were not hurt, they'd been put at risk by my foolishness. My breath came in short gasps. I was hyperventilating, something I never did in public. Typically, I saved panic for the privacy and darkness of my walk-in closet at home.

As police cars pulled up, I thought, *Oh God, I'll have to tell my parents. They'll be so disappointed. They already have enough to worry about with Willie, and I had to go ahead and do this?*

That's when I heard her voice, slow and gentle: "May I sit with you?"

I looked up to see an older woman approaching. She was wearing church clothes; she had kind eyes and a gentle manner. I nodded, and she sat next to me on the curb.

"I was on my way to Mass and saw the accident. Are you OK?"

I couldn't speak.

"Oh, dear, of course you're not. How scary that must have been."

I nodded, swiping at the snot and tears on my face.

"May I stay for a few minutes and pray for you?" she asked.

"Yes," I choked out.

And so she put her arm around me and prayed. Her words blurred together, and an hour later I couldn't have repeated a thing that she said, but I had a deep impression of comfort and solace.

She stayed with me, sitting on the curb while I called home. She stayed with me until my parents' car pulled up. Then she gave my shoulder a final squeeze and disappeared.

OF COURSE, THE WISE and logical thing to do would have been to go home and rest, to give myself the kind of compassionate care that that stranger had offered me.

But that's not what we do when we're disconnected from ourselves and terrified of making mistakes. We don't go gently; instead, we drive ourselves mercilessly. So after the car crash, I insisted that my parents drive me to school so that I wouldn't miss my third-period science class.

Yes, that's right. After surviving a head-on collision and having an anxiety attack, I decided to carry on as though nothing had happened.

My mom and dad both tried to talk me out of it, but I didn't listen. To my way of thinking, I'd already screwed up by getting in the accident, so I couldn't let myself fail again by missing school. That would be one mistake too many.

How does a teenage girl get to the place where she believes she's not allowed to make mistakes?

In my case, it took years of perfectionism on my part and serious behavioral issues on Willie's. Then there was a cultic church, abuse, trauma, and relational dysfunction. By the time I crashed the car, pushing past my limits and ignoring my body's signals was normal;

I'd been doing it for years. Yet even as I insisted on heading to school that day, I sensed I was crossing an invisible line.

A small voice within me whispered, *Honey, you have a problem.*

DOES THIS SOUND FAMILIAR?

We show up as problem-solvers, yet in our secret hearts, we fear that we *are* the problem. *What's wrong with you?* is the shaming mantra in our minds. Deep down we wish that we were allowed to be human— to make a mistake, to cry in public, to reschedule appointments when we're sick instead of pushing through the way we always do. But we believe that others' needs are more important than our own, so we show up for them even when we're exhausted.

We sense that there must be a better way, but we don't know how to break through our limiting beliefs to find it. We believe the lie that trying harder will save us, when in truth it keeps us stuck in the same patterns. And frankly, we do not want to look at the past pain that caused us to develop our favorite coping mechanisms. Our people-pleasing and perfectionistic patterns arose from old, emotional-level hurts, and who wants to feel those? So we seek out surface-level fixes. People tell us to make "simple" changes: *Just take it easy! Just give yourself grace! Just learn how to politely decline an invitation!* But it feels impossibly foreign. All of this good advice just doesn't translate to our felt experience.

We do our best to fix problems such as overwork and over-responsibility. But we never see lasting change by trying harder and working more. Here's why: we're not addressing our problem where it originated. We're caught in the impasse of wrapping our minds around emotional-level issues. We're trying to reason our way out of deep fear, and it simply doesn't work. Much like those who struggle with substance abuse, we're operating in response to unhealed trauma— we just pretty it up.

Perfectionism, people-pleasing, codependency, and constant striving to measure up—all of these patterns are rooted in fear and angst, which are emotional-level issues. The challenge for us is to bring love to the parts of ourselves that are hurting and terrified. Our work is to bridge the gap between the head and the heart.

This book isn't about the quick fix. It's not about changing one unhealthy pattern on the surface, then seeing the unresolved pain show up in some other area of our lives. (Ever seen someone who stops overeating and then takes up smoking a hot second later?)

Let's go gently into our original pain instead. Our problematic patterns arose to protect us from that pain. But if we are willing to (gradually) venture into the hurt, then we will have the opportunity to heal it.

When we heal the hurt, we don't need the addictions anymore. We are free to let go of the need to fix and save others, the people-pleasing, and the perfectionism.

To do this work, we need a compassionate witness, someone who holds space for our suffering.

Rather than providing you more ways to "effort" and effect change—which you've tried before—this book offers you something different. It's a kind of compassionate witness, a series of stories and situations in which you can glimpse your own reflection. In this way, the book asks for your participation. It invites you to enter into your own questions, your own stories, at a deeper level.

Each person's story is different and unique, yet on a deeper level, our struggles are similar. We share the desire to belong, to be loved, to accept ourselves as we are. In the same way that the woman on her way to Mass comforted me and prayed for me after my car accident, I offer you a safe space here.

But safe spaces can also be rousing wake-up calls, and I hope this book sounds an alarm for you as well. Each chapter title begins with a challenge, a daring phrase that helped shock me awake. I hope these challenges help you too; I hope they jolt you out of your old, harmful patterns and encourage you to claim your freedom. As you read, I would love for you to raise your voice along with me, to see how it feels to say, "I don't owe anyone!"

In the book's opening stories, I examine what it looks like for us to stay stuck in the try-hard cycle. I give voice to the fear that underlies perfectionistic striving, self-harm, and intense anxiety. I share tough stories from my own life, accounts of abuse and trauma. These dark times aren't about victimization, though; I share them to help you connect to your own resilience and appreciate all that you've already survived. These chapters also illumine the positive purpose of past pain (which is much clearer in hindsight). Then in later chapters, I share stories of overcoming dysfunctional patterns and learning new, healthier ways of being. Throughout each chapter, I unpack solutions for you. I show you what it looks like to refuse to overfunction in the old ways, and I invite you to make the same surprising choices that helped me get unstuck.

Every chapter concludes with an invitation to complete an exercise, a single suggested task to help you integrate what you've read. As a coach for recovering perfectionists, I've seen the power of these exercises firsthand. These tools have empowered me and clients to heal our hearts, allay our fears, and live with integrity. It's my hope that they will do the same for you.

THE NO-OWE INVITATION

Do Nothing, Every Single Day (Yes, Really)

In this first (and perhaps most challenging) coaching exercise, I welcome you—the Try-Hard Champion—to do nothing, daily. You will be tempted to dismiss and avoid this invitation. Don't. Instead, set a timer for fifteen minutes per day, and just be. Just sit still and be present.

Some people call this meditation, but I follow the lead of master coach Martha Beck and call it "doing nothing" because it helps me release into rest. Remember that you don't have to be good at meditation. You just need to do nothing daily for at least one month and see what shifts in you.

If you're not used to stillness, the first few sessions may feel just awful. You may have a twitchy, crawling-out-of-your-skin feeling; you may feel a strong compulsion to get back on your feet and do something—anything! If you can, sit with the discomfort. Breathe through it.

That said, if it feels too intense to sit still, you may need to release stored energy first. One great way to do this is to simply let your body shake. Let your limbs tremble in whatever way they need to. (Personally, I find it easiest to shake my legs when I'm feeling too much charge, and I can do that even when I'm seated at my desk on a video call.) If you want more detailed instructions, there are some great free resources available; just look up "Trauma Release Exercises" or "TRE" online.

You may find that the first five minutes of "doing nothing" are the hardest and that it gets easier to be still after that. Or you may find that doing nothing feels like an uphill battle the entire time. Stick with it anyway. You are addicted to achieving, and you can go back to achieving when the fifteen minutes are up. But for now, you get to just be.

Often, clients will tell me that they don't have time to do this. I can relate to that. There have been long periods of my life when I've believed that I didn't have time to be still. But what I've found is that, in the end, none of us have time *not* to be still. If we don't slow down, we will invariably lose touch with who we are and drift off course from where we want to go.

When coaching clients come to me and say that they don't know what they want or that they feel lost, the first question I ask is, "How much time do you spend doing nothing?" Usually the answer is "None." Their frantic pace blocks access to their inner wisdom.

Many high achievers are scared to spend fifteen minutes in silence because they fear wasting time and losing productivity. In my experience, the opposite is true. If I take at least fifteen minutes to be still, I'm more focused, clear-headed, and present for the rest of the day.

So that's my charge to you: Spend daily time alone, doing nothing. Drop your efforts and your expectations. You're not doing this in order to get some grand spiritual epiphany. You're simply turning down the noise and tuning into the truth of your own life.

1

You Don't Owe Anyone
the Good Child

> The secret sorrows—and future difficulties—of the good boy
> or girl begin with their inner need for excessive compliance.
> The good child isn't good because by a quirk of nature they
> simply have no inclination to be anything else. They are
> good because they have no other option. Their goodness is a
> necessity rather than a choice.
>
> —The School of Life,
> "The Dangers of the Good Child"

IF YOU WERE THE good child and you've kept up your "good" status into adulthood, the secret truth is that you're *tired*.

Not just tired in the physical sense, though often that's true too. It's more like a deep-down weariness; your heart and soul feel spent.

This is what readers write to me:

"I try so hard to do everything right and not screw up. Caroline, do you know how exhausting that is? I think you do; that's why I'm writing to you."

They're right; I do know. I know how exhausting it is to be the good child, and I also know how it feels like an imperative. As in the epigraph to this chapter, I know what it's like when your goodness seems like "a necessity rather than a choice."

It's been your survival strategy for years, hasn't it? Just keep going, just keep fixing and saving. That's your job, isn't it? To help but not be helped?

To wit, another reader's message:

All my life I've been good at offering help to others, but I don't want to ask for or accept help myself. If I am able to do it on my own, then I should, right?

But I'm so tired. I can put on a fun-loving front some of the time, but lately it's getting harder. If I'm honest, I don't think I am worthy of love or companionship. Secretly, I think that I am a disappointment to my family and friends.

Getting honest about our fatigue is a first step. But however many self-help articles we read or commonsense solutions our friends offer, slowing down and resting feel wildly uncomfortable. We drive ourselves hard, it's true, but there's a familiar comfort in the fast pace. On some deep level, we believe that this is how life is supposed to be for us. And as a result, we keep going right up until the breaking point.

A reader at that critical juncture wrote to me: "I have had enough of living this way. I have a daughter who I hope does not turn into me. I want more for her than just going through the motions. I want her to live freely and without regrets. But how?"

When we want more for our children, it's time to take a closer look at our younger selves. It's time to look at their "secret sorrows" and hidden joys, to see life once more through their eyes.

WHEN I LOOK BACK at my first dance recital, I remember a shiny sequined costume and a belly full of butterflies. For a kindergarten girl, it was pretty much heaven.

I wore a bright-blue satin top trimmed with silver sequins and a stiff tutu. My ballet shoes, tights, and gloves were white. The sequined straps and choker made my chest and back itch, but they sparkled so much that I didn't care. The auditorium was dark, but the spotlights were bright. On stage I could see dust motes we kicked up and how the sequins from our costumes caught the light. I could hear the music and feel it in my body. Performing wasn't as scary as I thought it would be. In fact, it was fun!

At the end of the dance, I was in the front row, kneeling and then rising along with the other girls. But instead of pushing myself up from the floor with my hands like we'd practiced, I wrapped my hands around the microphone stand and used it to pull myself up. Then I sang the last words of the song right into the microphone. That improvisation came to me without thought; it just felt right. The audience clapped for us, and in that golden moment I felt like a real ballerina, like a star.

After the show, Mom and Dad found me in the front hall of the auditorium. Mom reached me first, and I felt the soft fabric of her floral dress against my cheek as she held me in a tight hug. She handed me a little bouquet of pale-pink plastic roses, saying, "For you, my beautiful daughter."

Flushed, I smiled up at her. In the packed hallway with the other dancers and their families, Mom smoothed my hair, tucking in a strand that had slipped from the hairspray-shellacked, heavily bobby-pinned bun she'd made hours before.

"My big girl! You were so confident up there! How did you get so grown up? Oh, we need to take a picture. Where's the camera?" She turned to my dad.

"Right here," he said, passing the camera to Mom and bending down to give me a quick side-hug. "Good job, Cari-Cat." He called me Cari-Cat because we liked the way it sounded and because my fondest dream was to have a cat of my own. At Dad's side, I felt both smaller and safer.

Since I'd learned about the solar system in school, I thought about our family members in celestial terms. If I was the earth, then Willie was the moon. He was the closest to me yet also quietly separate, in his own world. Dad was gravity, constant and steady but invisible while he was at work. And Mom was the sun, the bright, volatile fire at the center of everything.

When Mom held up the camera and said, "C'mon, sweetie, smile!" I showed as many of my teeth as I could and fought not to blink for the flash.

As I squinted away the blind spots, Mom raised her eyebrows and said, "Now really, honey, I have to ask: What on earth were you doing with the microphone? You couldn't get up by yourself?" Her tone turned scolding, critical. "Do you want people to think you had to use the stand to help you? It was just so ... *melodramatic*!" She shook her head in dismay, then softened a little. "Well, I guess you had to do it *your* way, huh?" Then she laughed, and Dad chuckled too.

My face burned. My stomach sank. I didn't know what *melodramatic* meant, but by the way Mom said it, I knew that it was not something that I was supposed to be. My teacher had not taught me to slide my hands on the microphone stand, but I had done it anyway, and I understood from Mom's words that it had been a bad decision.

Shame cast a pall over that bright evening; the excitement was gone and the fun was over. I had messed up, and the feeling inside of me was terrible.

DID YOU EVER HAVE a moment like that, when you thought you were OK—doing well, even—and then you felt a cold bucket of water thrown over the experience? Ever stood with your family and pretended to feel fine when inside, you were drenched in shame?

It's akin to playing a video game like *Super Mario Bros.* for the first time. Chances are, you start off feeling relaxed about the whole thing. *Oh, this is silly, but this is fun! Look how high I can jump!* You learn to operate the controls while your character stumbles and flails around, and you laugh at your own ineptitude.

But when you're a kid and you gain even a little bit of mastery—and get a few well-timed criticisms from the authority figures in your life—then what happens? You stop goofing off. All at once, there are expectations. You have to *perform*. If you do well on one round and then flub the next, you're disappointed (and perhaps so are the people around you). The game becomes both more interesting and more intense because you are invested in it. It feels good to win and even better not to lose. You fight to gather up the gold coins; you do whatever you need to do to stay alive.

You love the thought of doing well, and you dedicate yourself to that pursuit. You work hard to avoid flubs and mistakes, and when they do happen, you try your best to hide them. Gradually, you forget how it was when you started. You forget that you were only ever playing a game.

Does that feel like the story of our lives or what? We start out fumbling around, just playing and having fun. That's our job as children. But then at some point, we get the message that life is very serious business. We are asked to be good, to say yes, to respond as the grown-ups expect. And some of us get the sense that making a mistake equals death.

We carry this attitude forward into our adult lives—we've got to keep going, keep hustling, make sure we never slip! Yet the irony is that while we're running scared, both the video game universe and the real world are more generous than we think. We believe that we must enact a perfect performance, but the truth is that if we miss a step, we can choose to restart and begin again.

Anne Lamott says that "perfectionism is based on the obsessive belief that if you run carefully enough, hitting every stepping stone just right, you won't have to die." To some people, a statement like that sounds hyperbolic. Surely no one walks around feeling that kind of pressure! But you and I know better. We know what it's like to believe that we owe the world the Good Child.

Nobody gets through this life unscathed. All of us have had times of trouble; as the saying goes, everyone has a story that would break your heart. For some of us growing up, it was the struggle for financial survival. Some of us lived in communities so disadvantaged that perfectionism was our only way to order our worlds. I want to be clear, dear reader: from the moment I was born, I had a head start. Parents who wanted children. A nice house on a quiet, suburban street. Good public schools. White privilege. Money for dance lessons for me and early intervention therapies for Willie.

I was fortunate—there is no question about it. But still, the soundtrack of deep fear accompanied me throughout childhood. Good fortune and fear are not mutually exclusive. It has taken me decades to understand that, but it's true. I was lucky, and I was afraid.

How can this be?

To answer that question, we need to talk about the true nature of trauma. Specifically, we need to talk about the difference between physical and psychological trauma. Physical trauma involves injury to the body, such as a broken bone. It's medical and mostly measurable. There's a fairly straightforward connection between cause and effect. (If you're cut, you bleed.) Psychological trauma, on the other hand, is entirely subjective. It's all about how a given circumstance registers for you personally. If an event was hurtful and shocking to you—if it led you to believe that it wasn't safe for you to be yourself—then it was traumatic for you. Period. No one else gets to judge. No one else gets to tell you that it doesn't count or that it wasn't real. If it was scary and shocking within you, then it counts as trauma.

Two people can encounter the same external event and have very different internal experiences. For example, another little girl might have heard her mother's words about being melodramatic during her dance recital and brushed them off or forgotten them. But I didn't. My mother was the sun around which I orbited. I took her every word to heart, and *melodramatic* hurt. Whenever my mom spoke critically, I made myself a rule: I would do whatever it took so that I'd never have to hear those words again. I'd do anything to avoid the darkness I felt when the sun turned her bright beams away.

DO YOU KNOW WHAT it's like to orient yourself around other people's approval, to seek it like sunshine? For those of us who were addicted to gold stars, elementary school could be a reassuring place.

All we needed to do was follow the rules, and we got our fix: positive reinforcement, validation, and a sense of safety, however temporary. Good grades meant that we were not about to fall off the face of the earth.

Small wonder, then, that I was a good student. By the time I was in first grade, my worksheets always came back with "Excellent!" on the top. For me, words of praise went into the same sweet category as cupcakes and shortbread jelly cookies. They were my favorite things, worth every effort to obtain.

But one fateful day, my first grade teacher, Mrs. Summers, returned my paper with "See Me" written in red ink. Getting a "See Me" meant lining up by Mrs. Summers's desk and waiting to talk to her privately, in front of everyone. For a girl like me, this meant adding the public shame of being corrected to the private awfulness of making a mistake.

At "See Me" time, I slunk to the back of the line. I stared down at my pink T-shirt, floral-print leggings, and Keds sneakers and tried very hard not to cry. Even the usual trick of running ribbons of my soft, brown hair around my fingers didn't help. (If you have ever fought tears in an elementary-school classroom, then you know just how desolate I felt.)

When my turn came, Mrs. Summers took one look at me and said, "Caroline, dear, what's wrong?"

Unable to speak, I handed her my paper and waited for the worst.

"Sweetie, listen. Do you know why I wrote 'See Me' on your paper?"

I shook my head woefully. "No!" I croaked. Tears ran down the sides of my face. I'd gone over and over it, and still I couldn't find the mistake.

"It's because you did a great job, and I just wanted to tell you that in person. That's all! Do you understand?"

I nodded, and she put her arm around my fragile, shaking shoulders.

"Caroline, it's OK. It's OK! I'm sorry I scared you. It's all right—you're doing a great job!"

Hearing those words felt like that moment in a video game when you think you're going to die, and then at the last second, you land on a mushroom or a coin and realize that you're saved.

From then on, I loved Mrs. Summers. I loved her the way I loved my water wings; I loved her for not letting me sink. And when she announced that our class would be making books, I couldn't believe my good fortune. Making books! I'd craved books before I'd known how to read them, chasing my mom around the house pleading, "Read! Read!" This was right up my alley.

Mrs. Summers told our class, "You'll each need to write about ten sentences and then do drawings. It will take time, but I'll help you, don't worry. When you're done, you'll have your pictures pasted on the inside covers too, just like real authors. Do you know what an author is? An author makes books as their job!"

An author. What could be better than that? Right then, I knew I wanted to be one.

What was your moment, dear reader, when you knew what direction you wanted to take, what path your soul wanted to pursue? Did you have a sense of awe and wonder? *Wow, there's actually a job description for the thing I think is the coolest thing in the world. And there's a possibility, however remote, that I could do it!*

Or perhaps you were simultaneously delighted by the dream and daunted by the work that lay ahead. If you were lucky, you had a teacher, coach, or mentor who helped you take the next small step and move through the overwhelm.

Mrs. Summers coached our class, "If you're not sure what to write about in your book, choose something that is important to you."

Something important to me—Willie! I'll write about Willie. On the book cover, I drew a stick-figure boy wearing a boxy red shirt and rectangular green pants. He had no hands or feet, just pencil-thin arms and legs and a dash of red crayon for a smile. Above my stick-figure brother I added a cotton-puff cloud and a sun with big yellow rays.

"My brother's name is Willie," my book began. "We do things together like jump on the bed and wake up at six o'clock and wake Mom and Dad up." Stick-figure Mom and Dad smiled; in my book, they seemed happy to see us so early.

In my book, I detailed Willie's love for dinosaurs, playing outside, and lining things up in rows. Repeating both what our parents had told me and what I'd observed, I wrote, "My brother likes to be alone most of the time." With the bracing honesty of childhood, I added, "I love to play with him *sometimes*."

WHAT I DIDN'T WRITE in the book is that we called our favorite game "Run away." It involved running laps through the first floor of our house, shrieking and giggling as Mom or Dad pursued us, or we pursued each other. It was exhilarating to run and be chased, to play a game with Willie that he liked and understood just as I did.

Willie didn't need encouragement to run. He bolted so often that when we went out to crowded places, Mom would hook him up to a little rainbow leash like a puppy so that he wouldn't disappear into the crowd. Even when we were at home, Willie would slip out the door and escape periodically. He'd be halfway to the park before anyone realized he was gone.

When that happened, Mom would call me to our gray Volvo. As she pulled onto the road, she would coach me in her *I'm just barely holding it together* voice, "Keep your eyes open! Keep looking, and try to find him!"

I'd try hard not to blink so that I wouldn't miss a glimpse of Willie. When we finally discovered him, Mom would pick him up and strap him into the back seat with me, then talk with the police officers if they'd found him first. Once I had my brother seated next to me, I'd feel an ice-cream swirl of feelings: mad mixed with glad, with sprinkles of *I'm the good kid* superiority on top.

I couldn't spare my parents. I couldn't give them time off from caring for Willie. But what I could do was try to shine, to give them less to worry about where I was concerned. I thought that I owed them that much.

OFTEN OUR EARLY COPING mechanisms—the ones that feed into perfectionism—seem positive and altruistic. And in a way, they are. They're our best attempts to help, to fix, to make things right with the world. We try so hard because we care so much. We care about our people; we want to make life better for those we love. That's not bad! The trouble comes when we chase perfection at the expense of our own humanity. We give our loved ones permission to make all kinds of mistakes, yet we deny ourselves that same freedom.

As I worked hard to do everything right, to get "Excellent" on all of my worksheets, I witnessed Willie's relative disinterest in acing his lessons. In my little book, I wrote, "He hates to do his speech lesson with my mom and dad. He hates to be yelled at." I drew a picture of Willie looking at a desk with wide, anxious eyes, and I sketched our mother with a "NO!" word bubble coming from her mouth. "My parents spend most of their time teaching him," I wrote. "I go to my friends' house while this is going on."

To be sure, I had fun at my friends' house; I lived next door to two girls about my age, and the three of us watched *Saved by the Bell* and daydreamed about going out to diners and wearing neon pants and crop tops. But on the occasional afternoons when I didn't go next door while Mom and Willie were doing speech therapy and Dad was out working, I had this empty feeling inside of me that I couldn't explain. It was as though I was on a raft by myself in the middle of the ocean with nothing on the horizon for hundreds of miles.

In my book, I was matter of fact about the truth of our life. Willie needed Mom and Dad more. That was the way things were. And even as I implied that it wasn't easy to have a younger brother with autism, I ended the book this way: "I love my brother so much I could run through the wall!" At six years old, I was able to express exactly how I felt about Willie: I loved him enough to do the impossible.

MY GUESS IS THAT this desire to do the impossible is familiar to you. I'm guessing that you decided to aim for it too. That's what we do, isn't it? We aim for the impossible—for perfection—and then castigate ourselves for failing.

For so many of us, this story became our anchor, our internal rule: *I owe them the Good Child. This is who I have to be, no matter how scared I feel inside.*

Then we carry this rule forward into our future lives. Even as our situations change, even as we grow up and move away from home, there's a part of us that believes we must be "better" and "stronger" than we actually are.

To be sure, this usually isn't a conscious choice. Consciously, we understand that we're human, that we're allowed to rest and relax our old hypervigilance. We love the idea that we're grown up, that we're free to make our own choices and go out to diners, finally! Subconsciously, however, we're still in survival mode.

—

DURING MY FIRST WEEK as a freshman at Vassar College, one of my hall mates caught me folding my dirty laundry. My hall mate was an athletic, popular, outgoing guy from Long Island. He walked into the room I shared with two other girls just in time to see me—a shy, introverted, Bible-toting girl from New Jersey—folding my duck-decal pajamas and placing them in the mesh hamper at the foot of my bed.

It was, in a word, embarrassing.

Of course, I didn't want anyone to know that I folded my dirty laundry. I didn't understand why I did it, why I had this impulse that drove me to tidy compulsively.

Much later, I learned that in the Enneagram personality framework, the Type 1 Perfectionist's knee-jerk response to stress is to bring order to the physical world as much as possible. Some people read Marie Kondo's book *The Life-Changing Magic of Tidying Up* and thought that it was too intense. Personally, I found it soothing. Corralling all clothing items into one place before sorting them? Rolling up socks into tidy, sushi-style bundles? Yes, please!

As a college freshman, though, I didn't want my peers to know how neurotic I was. So I flushed with embarrassment when my hall mate called me on it: "Hey, Caroline, did you *seriously* just fold those pajamas before you put them into your hamper?"

His tone was more amused than accusatory; he was a decent guy, not given to tormenting people. Even so, I felt the old, awful wave of shame crest over me. I felt like hiding under the bed.

"Oh, um, yeah," I choked out, aiming for insouciance and missing by a wide margin. "I did. You got me. I'm a total neat freak," I said, trying to laugh it off.

He smiled and let it go, turning to ask my roommate whether she'd made the lacrosse team. I swallowed hard and tried to push aside the critical voice inside my head that said, *You're so weird! Why can't you be normal? What's wrong with you?*

As a college freshman, I thought that if I could just get everything lined up exactly right, then I'd feel safe. Yet oddly enough, my hidden source of comfort that year was a so-called imperfection.

Long after I stopped folding dirty laundry and settled into life at school, I kept a different secret. Along the wall next to my single bed was a painted-over star sticker. It was affixed to the wall just above the wooden chair rail; it was a small imperfection, easily missed. Every night when I went to sleep, I reached out my hand and ran my fingers over that crooked little star. I felt along the raised edges with my fingertips, and it gave me a shot of strength every time.

That star wasn't supposed to be there. Some dorm inspector had overlooked it, and some painter had swished a haphazard brush over it. It was a mistake, something you'd think would bother a card-carrying perfectionist. My mind might have categorized it as a mistake, but my heart believed it was supposed to be there. My heart believed it was supposed to remind me of the painted-over stars on the ceiling of my childhood bedroom. The star was supposed to remind me that no matter how small and scared I felt, in some fundamental way, I was safe.

And somewhere between folding my dirty laundry and grazing my fingertips against that secret star at college, I encountered the poem "Wild Geese" by Mary Oliver. The opening line—"You do not have to be good"—was like a cannon fired at close range. I felt it reverberate in my body; it thrilled and terrified me all at once. Shame was suffocating, and this was pure oxygen.

That line, that poem, that little star—these things were like the woman who stopped on her way to Mass and sat with me the morning of my car accident. They were touches of grace when I needed them most.

WHETHER YOU "PUT YOUR world in order" by folding your dirty laundry or reading books on organization or simply shoving clutter into a closet, it doesn't matter. What matters is learning how to be kind to yourself.

I know this isn't easy. I know what it's like to live steeped in self-judgment, to be so hard on yourself that it hurts. Even so, I invite us both to make the shift from self-judgment to self-compassion. This looks like putting down the dirty laundry and letting our fingers graze the star instead. It's about letting go of control and holding on to wonder.

Before we can do that, though, we need to comfort the frightened, vulnerable parts of ourselves. We need to come face-to-face with the aspects of our lives we've been covering up with hard work and fierce self-control.

Choosing compassion in adulthood means listening to that childhood self, bearing witness to her truths, and offering her kindness. It means looking at her with a gentler gaze, seeing that she's just a kid struggling with a world out of order.

Children's narratives are, by nature, incomplete and overly simplified interpretations of reality. (So are adults', for that matter.) When confusing things happen to us as children, we create stories to make sense of the inexplicable. But our brains aren't fully developed yet, and neither are our narratives. One of the most popular childhood stories is "If anything bad happens, then it is all my fault."

And of course, the close cousin of that story is "If I can just get it right, then it will all be OK."

Ergo, perfectionism.

If you're struggling with perfectionism, it doesn't mean that you're hopeless or bad. It means that you're human, and at some point you were hurt. When that happened, the Good Child role became your refuge, your necessity. Given what you knew and believed at the time, it was the best that you could do.

It's tempting to skim over the hurts of the past. It's easy to sugarcoat or dismiss them with that classic line: "Oh, it doesn't matter anymore; it was a long time ago." But when we don't acknowledge or heal those hurts, they keep driving our actions and causing us pain in the present. And we miss the chance to look closely at the meaning we made from them.

Time alone doesn't heal all wounds. Only love can do that. And when we apply love and acceptance to the parts of ourselves that hurt, we heal.

⸺

SO HOW DO YOU move forward now as an adult?

It starts with treating yourself as your own beloved child.

For the woman who wrote to me, wanting a different future for her daughter, I said, "It starts with you. It starts with deciding that you're going to do the work of learning to accept yourself."

Usually, this means seeking help, which most of us only do when we are desperate. We ask for help when our usual coping strategies don't work, when we hit a wall of depression, anxiety, or panic. That's what happened to me in my early thirties, in the wake of a major crisis. I'd been to therapy before, but this was different; this time, I was willing to get more intensive support and go deep into inner work. With the support of compassionate counselors, I worked with the mental and emotional pain that fueled my perfectionism.

In the process, I took a closer look at that supposedly shameful dance recital. I began asking questions about the girl I was, questions I had never asked before: *Do you despise that little girl for doing what she did that night? Was she really being melodramatic, or just joyful? And if she was being dramatic—well, so what? She's only a little girl. Do you judge her for grabbing the microphone stand and daring to shine?*

As it turned out, I didn't.

Try this for yourself and see what happens. Go and find a picture of yourself when you were little. Really study it. Imagine that this child is your child. Imagine that you are her parent. Do you despise her for doing what she did, for making the choices that she made when she was scared and lonely?

I don't think so. I'm guessing there's at least a glimmer of compassion, a flicker of empathy.

If that's too much of a stretch, get a picture of your favorite animal. Maybe it's a dog that leaps with exuberance at the sight of you or a cat that curls up with you when you sleep. Allow yourself to feel all of the affection that you have for this being. Then try looking at your childhood self with this same fundamental respect, the same fierce tenderness. (When I first tried this experiment, I looked at my younger self the way I look at my cat Bootsie when she curls up next to me and purrs as I rub her ears.)

It's probably clear to you that this animal is good simply because it is itself.

Then ask yourself, *What if the same is true for me? What if I am whole even when I feel broken? What if my deepest reality is light, not darkness?*

It's so tiring to hate yourself, honey. Do you know why that is? Because it's exhausting to believe a lie. It's exhausting to believe the lie that you owe anyone the Good Child, because that isn't you. That isn't real.

Every loving thing that has ever happened to you was real. Everything else is just an illusion.

Go for the real thing.

THE NO-OWE INVITATION

Practice Opposite-Hand Writing

If you're in pain from hating yourself, it's time to send yourself some kindness. One way to do this is to practice opposite-hand writing, also known as nondominant-hand writing. It's a form of reparenting that empowers you to heal past hurts. When you use your nondominant hand to write, you engage your brain in a way that allows you to bypass the walls you put up around your emotions. I learned about this healing tool from the counseling team at The Clearing, when I worked for them as a freelance copywriter. But the opposite-hand writing practice actually originated with Lucia Capacchione, PhD, author of many books, including *The Power of Your Other Hand*.

Before you begin this practice, it's important to center yourself in loving energy. This will lay the energetic groundwork for every exercise that follows in this book. Center yourself by connecting to the energy of love within your body. As described earlier, one easy way to do this is to call to mind a beloved child or perhaps a pet that you love unconditionally. You may also picture a partner or a dear friend; choose any being for whom you feel free, untroubled affection. Imagine that being in your mind's eye and feel the love flowing between you.

Once you've established that energy to the best of your ability, set an intention to heal. Then take up a pen and paper to practice opposite-hand writing. Start writing with your dominant hand, which represents your adult self. Ask your inner-child self, "How are you?" Then switch to your nondominant hand and reply as the child within. Let whatever comes up come up. It will most likely surprise you, and that's OK. Continue the dialogue in the present tense for at least one page, and focus on providing the vulnerable child reassurance, praise, and love. Make sure to ask your inner child, "How do you feel now?" Connect to an actual feeling state such as fear, anger, grief, or happiness rather than to thoughts about the feeling state. (You can hear the difference between "I feel like I shouldn't be alone anymore" and

"I feel scared." The former is a mental-level judgment; the latter is a feeling.)

To sum up, prompts for your inner child include (but are not limited to) the following:

How do you feel now?
What's that like for you?
Tell me more about …
What would you like to do?
What do you want/need right now?

The role of the "parent" hand is to provide unconditional love in real time. With that in mind, write mostly in the present tense on both sides of the dialogue. (The child can talk/write about her own past if she wants, but the main idea is to connect with how that vulnerable part of you is feeling right now.) If the child expresses anger toward you, that's OK. Your job is to be a safe space, a container to hold all of that strong emotion. You might say, "I'm right here. I love you. You can feel as angry as you need to feel and it's OK. You have permission to feel all of the big feelings."

At the end of the dialogue, ask, "What do you need right now in order to feel loved and safe?" Most often, you'll find that the child needs to receive reassurance, comfort, and support. Follow through on the child's request and build trust. For example, if your inner child wants a hug, wrap your arms around yourself and imagine that you're holding her close, comforting her.

Sometimes children make requests that aren't realistic—that's normal! If your inner child wants a pony, for example, you don't necessarily need to acquire one today. However, listen to the child's desire and work with her to create a solution, such as going horseback riding soon. Keep the dialogue going until you find a way to honor and fulfill the need that's behind the request. Then have the adult make a clear plan—for example, "Let's take a drive and go see the horses this Saturday."

2

You Don't Owe Anyone

Your Spiritual Allegiance

> God is forgiveness—or so that particular story goes, but
> in our house God was Old Testament and there was no
> forgiveness without a great deal of sacrifice.
> —Jeanette Winterson, *Why Be Happy*
> *When You Could Be Normal?*

WHENEVER I COME TO Spirit looking for discernment or direction, she gives me this powerful directive: *Go where the life is.*

Should I say yes to this invitation or stay home? Should I read or watch TV? Should I reach out or sit in stillness? *Go where the life is.* Those five words give me permission to tap into what feels like life to me at any given moment. When I share that phrase with coaching clients, they often start using it right away, to great effect. It helps us all shift from pro/con lists and mental-level analysis to trusting intuition. It frees us to get to the heart of the matter.

But have you ever had a hard time seeing things that simply, that clearly? "Go where the life is" only works if you give yourself permission to feel how you actually feel rather than how you're "supposed" to feel. If you feel anxious a lot, then chances are good that you feel trapped between your true feelings and your sanctioned roles; as you ping-pong between them, your anxiety rises.

There are good reasons why it feels so difficult to "go where the life is." If you grew up attending a controlling church or learning from an authoritarian faith or family leader, this may strike a chord.

Early on, we were taught to judge ourselves for having normal human feelings and needs. In church, we learned that denying ourselves was the way to be good. We were taught to do as we were told, sit still, be quiet, and not ask questions. To not even have questions! Sadness was considered bad, and anger was even worse. So we pressed those feelings and needs down so that we could be "more spiritual" and "better" than we actually were. Since we learned—implicitly and explicitly—that we were not OK as we were, we needed to pledge allegiance to something outside of ourselves. If we pledged allegiance to the church, we gave it our time, our money, and our loyalty, because being a part of the collective meant that we would be safe.

But if people repress their questions and feelings and genuine needs, year after year, a kind of spiritual handicapping happens. People are left not knowing what to do on their own, because they've been trained to look to external authorities to gauge what's permissible, right, and true. They believe they owe "them" spiritual allegiance.

The grown-ups said that we were born sinful, and now we think that we can't trust the truth in our own hearts. If we can't trust our own truth, we will have a lot of trouble feeling confident in our decisions.

We may struggle to make even simple choices. When we work from a spiritual paradigm that says our gut feelings are wrong and bad, we're blocked from trusting our bodies' wisdom. As such, we rely heavily on our minds to discern which choice is best. But often that means that we are working with two conflicting value systems. For example, we may have heard that it's important to be honest, but also, always obey the rules!

The double bind is a big problem. When we do what is right according to one system, we do something wrong according to the other. This isn't only an issue with restrictive religious environments, of course, but in any environment with one set of rules that conflicts with or even directly contradicts another set of rules. Is it any wonder that we feel a nagging guilt no matter what choices we make?

I'M NOT PROUD OF this, but I've wasted a lot of time gripped by false guilt. One winter when I was in my late twenties, I felt guilty that my husband Jonathan and I decided to spend $11 on two boxes of silver-ball Christmas tree ornaments. As Jonathan and I stood in the check-out line with our ornaments—the first we'd ever purchased together—an old, familiar anxiety arose. Shifting from foot to foot, I looked around the store, gazing at the giant wreaths and aisles upon aisles of decorations. All of this excess, all of this consumerism, all in the name of Christmas! And we were part of it!

Never mind that our artificial tree was a hand-me-down from Jonathan's grandmother. Never mind that we could afford the ornaments or that we'd been looking forward to hanging them on our tree. Never mind that I'd spent years eager for a Christmas tree of my own. Guilt told me that we were doing something wrong by making this purchase. We were transgressing somehow.

See if you recognize the logic: We weren't doing the *exact right thing* with our money. There were better ways to spend that $11. We were being selfish. We really should donate $11—or more!—to charity instead. We didn't really need Christmas decorations, did we? No, we did not. Therefore, we should not have them. It was better to avoid the possible sin of the silver ornaments than to enjoy their beauty.

Jonathan didn't feel the same way. Both of us are frugal, but only one of us was taught by their childhood church that Christmas trees were "pagan" (read: bad) and therefore off-limits to "true believers."

So I spoke tentatively: "Um . . . should we really buy these? Maybe it's too much. I feel guilty. I could put them back. Maybe we should put them back?"

Jonathan paused. We'd agreed to shop for ornaments, so he had every right to be annoyed. Instead, he thoughtfully replied, "It seems like you feel guilty about a lot of things unnecessarily. So maybe guilt isn't a reliable indicator of whether you should do something."

"Fair point," I said.

In the days that followed, I took a closer look at the guilt that was my constant companion. When I did, I realized that the guilt was almost never about a specific item, purchase, or idea. The guilt was a symptom of a deeper issue. The real problem was that I didn't feel comfortable in my own authority, my own spiritual life. I believed that I owed my spiritual allegiance to the God of my childhood church—a god I knew would never approve of those Christmas ornaments. And as I stood in the store check-out line, that version of God shouted so loudly that I couldn't hear my own voice.

—

WHEN WE'RE SMALL CHILDREN, most of us take for granted that our parents and caregivers have the answers. The adults are the primary gods in our pantheon—the ones who know just what to do. When we're little, it's very important that we believe that our caregivers are capable. If they're not, then we're not safe.

So it's important to look back on our early lives and realize, *Wait a minute*, those authority figures weren't gods; they were only ever people like us. They could be hurt, confused, and afraid. They could need comfort and certainty. They could join a cult without knowing it.

I know this because that's what happened in my family.

In the wake of Willie's autism diagnosis, my mother and I both spent time thinking about spiritual matters. As I lay in bed at night, it came to me so clearly that there must be a heaven. In some wordless way, I knew that heaven would be a place where I could really talk with my brother. In heaven, I could ask him questions and he would always answer. I could ask Willie what he thought about when he stared into space. I could ask him why he loved to run away from home. More than anything, I wanted a window into Willie's mind and heart. I didn't tell anyone about my idea of heaven, but I held onto it with everything I had. It made me feel warm and safe. That was my experience of the divine post-diagnosis: a sense of safety and comfort in the dark.

Our mom, on the other hand, decided to go to church in the light of day. Before Willie's diagnosis, our family wasn't part of a church. But after we got the news, Mom started reading the Bible and leaving the house on Saturday mornings to attend services at the Worldwide Church of God, or WCG. At Christmas, Willie and I uncovered a wooden Noah's ark under the tree. Mom read us the Bible story while we marched matching pairs of zebras and giraffes up and down the boat ramp. I loved walking animals into the red-roofed ark, and Willie loved tipping them out. We played with the ark all day. Yet the look on Mom's face when she read us the Bible story made me feel nervous. Something I wouldn't have known then to call intuition told me, *If Mom is buying us Bible-story toys, this church thing is really serious. This year we didn't talk about Santa, just the Bible. I guess from now on, we'll hear different stories.*

Initially, Dad and Willie and I all went to church with Mom. But soon Dad and Willie started staying home while Mom and I went to church. Church ran for at least two hours each week, and Willie had a hard time sitting through services. So Dad and Willie would stay home and do yard work or take our dog Curley for a walk.

I would go to church with Mom and sit next to my new friend Marie. She and I would get fidgety too, passing tiny, folded-up notes until her mother would frown and shake her head at us. Chastened, I'd stop writing and pick at snags in my tights while the pastor preached from a podium with a circular, golden WCG seal.

In the center of the circle was a drawing of a lion, a boy, and a lamb standing close together. Underneath them were the words *The lion shall dwell with the lamb and a little child shall lead them in the world tomorrow—Isaiah 11:6.* The World Tomorrow was the WCG's version of heaven, and our pastors and elders spent a lot of time talking about it. Though the church membership was racially and ethnically diverse, the pastors and elders were usually white men, sometimes Black men, and never women. And the WCG's heaven had a lot more rules than my version did. There were all kinds of things you needed to do and be in order to qualify for admission.

"YES!" MARIE WHISPERED, FLIPPING through the satin-smooth pages of the hardcover hymnal to find the right page for our first hymn of the service. "I love this one!"

"Me too," I whispered back.

"Onward, Christian soldiers! / Marching as to war," I sang along with Marie, my softer voice nearly drowned out by her louder one. I felt so grown up sitting next to Marie; she was a year older than me and had been going to church much longer. If she loved a hymn, then I did too. If she took careful sermon notes, then so did I. Marie was petite, with wispy blondish hair, and she was as good at giving orders as I was at obeying them.

"Are your dad and Willie here?" Marie asked, leaning slightly toward me during the short instrumental between verses. By unspoken rule, there was no physical movement allowed during church songs—no swaying, no clapping, only poker-faced piety. And I knew for sure that we weren't supposed to be talking in the middle of the song. I looked over at Marie's mother to check that she wasn't watching us before I risked a reply.

"Oh . . . um . . . no," I said. "They stayed home this week."

I made it sound like they'd be back soon, but in my heart I knew better. I felt that specific guilt you feel when you're not exactly lying, but you're not quite telling the truth either.

If you were a "good child" in an intensely religious environment, then you know how quickly that guilty feeling became your new normal. You know how readily you picked up on unspoken rules, such as *Families should all come to church together every week.*

But even if that wasn't your experience, you might remember a time when you felt scared because one or two members of your family went a different direction from the rest. When you were young, your family was your universe. And if the planets spun out of orbit, then where did that leave your solar system?

I felt steadier when all of my family members were gathered together. That's why the third verse of that militant hymn was my favorite—I loved the lyrics "We are not divided, all one body we . . ."

As I sang those words, I pictured what would happen when Mom and I came home from church, when our family would have Chinese food takeout for dinner.

Dad would pull out the big card table, snapping the metal legs into place in the TV room. Then we'd pile onto the couch and watch *Star Trek: The Next Generation* on TV, cheering a little when the shiny silver Starship Enterprise appeared and Captain Jean-Luc Picard spoke about space, the final frontier. Willie would run in and out of the room, playing with his books and toys, leaving and then circling back. The crew of the Starship Enterprise would speed through the vast darkness of outer space, but I'd be warm and cozy and ever so safe. On Saturday mornings and afternoons—church time—our family was split down the middle. But on Saturday nights, we were undivided.

That day in church, the pastor talked about the importance of keeping Saturday as the true Sabbath. He spoke about being part of the One True Church and being spared the Lake of Fire. (This was the WCG's version of hell, and it was as terrifying as the World Tomorrow was beautiful.) Whenever I heard about the Lake of Fire, I worried that Dad and Willie weren't part of the One True Church, since they didn't come to services. Did that mean that they were destined for the Lake of Fire? My whole body recoiled from that idea, but still, I wondered.

As an adult, I was struck by these lines in Katherine North's *Holy Heathen*:

"This is the true cost of indoctrinating children. They come to mistrust their own perception so deeply that they can't tell the difference between real right and wrong. They lose access to their own discernment and no longer trust their own sense of reality. . . . Without that inner compass, they can only mimic what they hope will keep them safe."

Back then, I didn't trust my body's responses to the WCG's doctrines. I was taught that those teachings were right, and I was sinful, so what did I know?

If you grew up attending a church with dire doctrines—or if you attend one now—I invite you to take a closer look at those teachings. Rather than taking for granted that they must be true, ask yourself, *Does this idea actually feel right to me? How does my body respond when*

I think about it? Does a deep part of me recoil? Would I want this for someone I love?

Here's a bonus tip for those of you who have had the experience of being terrified by a religious tenet. When a spiritual system hangs an awful threat like hellfire over your head, it's helpful to ask, *Who does this benefit? Who profits from scaring us this way?*

Look upstream. There will always be someone who benefits.

I didn't understand this as a child, but as an adult, it's clear: keeping people afraid is highly lucrative. And back in the day, the WCG had a real handle on this game. Only a short time prior to when my family started attending the church, the organization upheld a three-tithe system. This system demanded that up to 20 percent of members' pretax income be tithed to the church, while another 10 percent of members' income was specifically allocated to their attendance at church-related festivals. Plus, members were asked to contribute additional "freewill offerings" on holy days.

Where did all of the money go? Some of it went to pay pastors and create fun summer camps for kids, but a lot of it went to help the rich get richer. The WCG's central leadership members spent lavishly, lining the walls of their central auditorium with rare pink onyx and buying private planes, while regular people gave until it hurt.

(The first time I wrote about this in a blog post, a reader wrote in with a two-word comment that hit me like a punch: "That's extortion.")

So watch where the money goes. And if a church or other organization attempts to isolate you from the rest of the world, pay close attention. Dividing people from their families and friends is a classic control tactic. When you're reliant upon a certain group for most of your social and emotional support, it's that much harder to leave.

When I was young, the WCG observed seven holy days outlined in the Hebrew scriptures, much as some Jewish communities do. But then the church took it further, decreeing that its members must give up other "worldly" holidays. No Christmas trees or presents were allowed, not even Bible-themed ones. The church taught that Halloween, Christmas, and Easter were pagan holidays and thus strictly off-limits. In his booklet *The Plain Truth about Christmas*, the WCG's founder claimed that the Christmas tree was "termed by the Eternal as 'the way of the heathen.'"

You can imagine the guilt I felt when I went to my paternal grandparents' house at Christmas, when I saw all of the holiday trimmings and secretly adored them. I loved the wreath on the door and the glittery, gilded Christmas cards my grandparents hung from the ceiling of their front room. Most of all, I loved the beautiful Christmas tree, and I snatched stealthy glances at it when Mom wasn't looking. None of the red-and-green-wrapped presents under the tree were meant for Willie and me, though. I felt a pit in my stomach when the other grandchildren opened their Christmas gifts, but I didn't talk about that. I already knew what Mom would say: We were called to be different from the rest of the world. And we had our own holy days, after all!

Mom had talked me through the meaning of each holy day and God's plan of salvation for His chosen people. She'd illustrated each holy day on a paper banner, which she'd hung in the front hall of our house to help me memorize them. That banner was meant to be our road map; those holidays were our answers. How would we get through the year? This way, by this path. So many questions and unknowns surrounded Willie's autism diagnosis—*Was this or that early intervention therapy effective? What would Willie's future be?*—but the paper provided a clear path through the year. It was a strict sort of solace.

———

CULTS AREN'T SOLELY CHARACTERIZED by unusual beliefs, though often that's part of their makeup. Rather, cults are all about control. Be it covert or overt, cults seek to shut down their members' critical thinking and autonomy. In this spirit, cults may claim that they have a corner on The Truth and that everyone outside the organization is misguided. There's an odd double bind surrounding evangelism too; though members may be asked to invite friends, there's a sense of secrecy surrounding the cult, an implication that people on the outside just won't "get it."

Again, cults keep people's worlds small. They subtly or explicitly separate their members from so-called outsiders, from the people in their lives who aren't part of the fold. They narrow their members' focus until this one community fills their entire frame and becomes their sole support system. Having different holidays was one way that WCG kept families separate from the rest of the world. It was effective; after a while, only church friendships seemed real to me. My church friends and I would talk about how kids at school seemed strange to us and how much we'd come to rely on each other. After all, who else could understand what it was like to skip Santa-themed crafts and only lip-sync the words to Christmas carols during holiday concerts? Who else our age knew what it was like to lead a double life?

Halloween was another distancing. All day at school I'd see everybody else's bright disguises and felt lost and left out. The bass drumbeat of my heart was *Why not me? Why can't I?*

When I begged to be allowed to march along with my class in the elementary school's Halloween parade, the way I had before we attended the WCG, Mom didn't bend.

"Sweetie, I'm sorry, but no," Mom said. "Remember, we don't celebrate Halloween anymore."

"But why not?" I pressed. "It's just like a game of dress-up."

"Well, Cari, Halloween isn't a holiday that honors God. It's a pagan holiday, and it glorifies bad things like witchcraft. We're God's people, remember? God's people are called to be separate from the world."

Mom spoke with firm, closed-door finality, and I understood that there would be no more Halloween parades in my future. The message was clear: church doctrine mattered more than feelings. And the whole "separate from the world" thing was already working—when I told my classmates that my church wouldn't let me celebrate Halloween, they said that it was weird. They didn't understand the doctrine, and I didn't know how to explain it to them.

Furrowing my brow, I risked asking my mom, "What about the other kids? If they wear costumes, are they in trouble with God?"

"Oh, honey, you don't need to worry," she said. Her voice turned gentle, soothing. "God knows what He's doing. Other people just haven't been called yet. I'll tell you what, though. I bought some candy for the trick-or-treaters who come to our door. You can help by handing it out."

It wasn't nearly as much fun as the trick-or-treating we'd done before. But after a while, I started to feel almost proud. Handing out candy, I thought, *I don't need to dress up and do foolish, worldly things like the other kids. I am a Christian soldier.*

———

KIDS ARE FAST LEARNERS, and they have astonishing powers of adaptation. Expose them to something long enough and even the wackiest stuff acquires a kind of uncomfortably comfortable normalcy. And again, cults and other dysfunctional systems discourage close relationships with outsiders, thereby depriving their members of alternative perspectives. This lack of spiritual diversity is harmful for everyone, but it's particularly problematic for kids. When children are taught to think in black and white early on, it's harder for them to shift those patterns later in life. (Don't worry, it's not impossible; I coach clients on this process every day. You just need to create new neural pathways, which takes some time and practice.)

My story is somewhat unusual, but all of us know what it is to adapt to a dysfunctional system to some degree. Be it a family, friendship, church, or culture, all of us have spent time in unhealthy, controlling dynamics. I emphasize this at the risk of sounding obvious, because I know what it's like to torture oneself with *I should have known better.* There have been times when I've slipped into the belief that surely no one else would have fallen for that garbage dressed up as the will of God; surely other people would have seen the craziness sooner.

But the truth is that even though the WCG taught me to think in black and white, the experience itself *wasn't* all good or all bad. Yes, the sermons were long and the doctrines despicable, but I loved whispering with my friends and racing through the halls, expending all our pent-up energy after services. I loved meeting people who had different skin colors and different stories to tell, loved how we became family in some deep and wordless way. I loved feeling a part of something sacred, the way I did when we all sang together.

And again, adaptation is really powerful.

Martha Beck said it well in *Leaving the Saints*:

"It wasn't slavery, but it was a powerful form of bondage: the belief that God had ordained a pattern of secrets and silence, that religious authority always trumped one's individual sense of right and wrong, that the evidence of the senses must bow to the demands of orthodoxy, no matter how insane."

And so it took me more than twenty years to understand just how crazy-making it was for me to cast myself as a Christian soldier when I was just a kid who wanted to go trick-or-treating. The epiphany came when I was thirty-one, as I was walking out of a group counseling session with a handful of new friends. Someone made a comment about childhood church craziness, and suddenly I heard myself talking. Since I felt safe, the words just came out, unbidden.

I told them about the WCG, about how holidays like Halloween had pagan origins and were therefore deemed "bad." I told them about being taught to not be "of the world."

"One year," I said, "I was allowed to dress up and go trick-or-treating, but the next year I wasn't allowed, because of the church. But my parents wanted to be neighborly or something, so they had me hand out candy to other kids who came to our door."

I kept my eyes down as I spoke, but when I looked up, the whole group was staring at me.

The guy I trusted most spoke first, with great emphasis and energy: "That is *so* fucked up!"

My eyes widened; his reaction astonished me. I was so accustomed to this memory that I didn't expect anyone else to be shocked by it. In that moment, I realized how much I'd curated my childhood stories to help me cope. "You think so?"

"Um, *yes*," he said. "Having a kid hand out candy to other kids on Halloween and not letting her trick or treat? That is fucked up. That is just . . . *wrong*."

Everyone else in the group nodded. These friends weren't easily stunned. They'd dealt with drug addiction, depression, and sexual abuse. If they thought it was messed up, it was. I looked from face to face, finding equal combinations of outrage and compassion in their expressions.

And I haven't even told them about Christmas, I thought.

In that moment, something inside of me unlocked. All at once, I could see what my friends saw. I caught a glimpse of a different reality, one in which what I'd missed out on actually *was* a big deal. Instead of guilt, I felt healthy, warranted anger. I wanted to smash things, yell, and rage for the little girl I'd been, the one who was forbidden a Christmas tree and a costume and encouraged to be a Christian soldier instead.

"You're right." My voice grew louder and stronger. "It was." I took a deep breath and let loose: "It *was* fucked up."

In that moment, strong language was the only language that fit. I'd spent so long minimizing, glossing over, and putting a positive spin on things. What a sweet relief it was to simply acknowledge that my younger self—and even my adult self!—cared about costumes and Christmas trees. How wonderful it was to let myself know my own truth: that I'd missed out, and that it *mattered*.

It was the shift from the collective, Christian-soldier truth to my truth. It felt deeply subversive, and it also felt great. In that moment, I sensed that I didn't owe anyone my spiritual allegiance except myself.

IF YOU TYPICALLY HAVE a hard time getting angry on your own behalf—though you feel guilty at the slightest possible infraction—then know this: there's nothing wrong with you. The false guilt is a survival mechanism and a trauma adaptation. If your internal "guilt gauge" is overly responsive, then you're going to feel a real guilt onslaught when you start setting healthy boundaries and taking better care of yourself.

As Dr. Gabor Maté wrote in *When the Body Says No*, "For many people, guilt is a signal that they have chosen to do something for themselves. . . . 'I feel guilty?' [one] could say. 'Wonderful. Hallelujah! It means I must have done something right, acted on my own behalf for a change.'"

What helped me most was recognizing a corollary to what Jonathan said when we went shopping for ornaments: if I couldn't look to my guilt gauge for a reliable reading, if I was going to feel guilty no matter *what* I did, then I might as well go ahead and make some positive changes! I might as well go ahead and set healthy boundaries and take good care of myself.

As it turns out, I don't have to let false guilt run my life, and neither do you. You can feel it, survive it, and practice making different choices. You can acknowledge the guilt, allow it to be there, and maybe even thank it for how it has kept you safe in the past. And then you can go ahead and do what feels right to you now.

If you're scared to feel more guilt, that's OK. You don't have to do anything before you're ready. You are allowed to go gently with this process. (My favorite guideline for inner work comes from a therapist quoted in Anne Lamott's novel *Blue Shoe*: "Go only as fast as the slowest part of you [can] go.")

So if you are afraid to feel the guilty feelings, practice being kind to the parts of you that are afraid. If a part of you is afraid to go gently because darn it, you need to change now! . . . then be kind to that part too. Allow the resistance. When you resist the resistance, it only gets worse.

Instead, take the frightened part of you into your metaphorical arms.

When you do, you may find that a strange and wonderful thing happens: you remember the magic you thought you'd lost.

That's what happened to me, at least. That day at the ornament store, Jonathan coached me through my guilt and second-guessing, and we bought those silver ornaments after all. Then we hung them on our hand-me-down artificial Christmas tree. We replaced the burnt-out lights and wrapped new strands around the fake pine needles.

When I stepped back and looked at the whole spectacle, I thought, *You, dear Christmas tree, are everything I was taught to turn my back on. You are unnecessary and frivolous. And based on this faded price tag I found in your branches, you were expensive too. And in my eyes, you are beautiful.*

One of the gifts that my WCG childhood gave me is the ability to connect just about everything to a biblical passage. As I gazed at our tree, I remembered the story of a woman pouring expensive perfume on Jesus. The religious leaders were angry at that woman. They protested that the perfume should have been sold and the proceeds given to the poor. What decadence, to "waste" it all on Jesus! In other words, *What a Christmas tree!*

I smiled then, remembering what Jesus had supposedly said to the critics: "'Leave her alone. . . . Why are you bothering her? She has done a beautiful thing to me.'"

I pictured myself back in the store, and I felt Spirit say, "Get out of here, guilt! Why are you bothering Caroline? She is decorating a tree with her husband, just like she's always wanted. She's doing what she can to move beyond her past and create some happiness here and now. Leave her be. What she's doing is beautiful."

———

THOSE OF US WHO survived abusive religious or family systems with our spirits intact had to keep secrets in order to stay sane. We had to hold on to quiet dreams of a better way amid the brokenness.

Even though I followed all of the WCG's rules and bought into the doctrine with my mind, a well of truth remained in my heart. As a little girl, I dreamed about heaven as a place with no barriers between people, a place where my brother and I could understand each other perfectly. Back then, I didn't know that I could trust that childhood vision more than any external system of authority. For so many years, I didn't know that I could pledge allegiance to my own truths. After that pivotal conversation with my friends after therapy, though, I spent time writing about how I really felt during those childhood holidays. I stopped protecting other people's feelings and wrote about what it was like to be me.

In the process, I realized that although Willie's diagnosis helped bring our mom to the WCG, it was life with Willie himself that kept a small, healthy seed of doubt alive in my heart. Even as I'd kept the regimented rules of the church, I'd always wondered, *If a person has to obey all of the rules to be saved with the firstfruits, then what does that mean for my brother, who as far as I know can't understand all of these complicated doctrines?* There had always been a bedrock part of me that would never accept a God who rejected my brother. It was the same part of me that knew that there was nothing wrong with dressing up for Halloween with my classmates.

When we access those truthful places as adults, we may be in for a lovely surprise. We may discover that God (or Spirit, or the Universe, or Goddess, or whatever name feels right to you) never needed us to feign invulnerability. Instead, we may find that this Being is proud of us for being honest. When we listen closely to Spirit, we may find Someone who cares about our hurts and wants us to enjoy good things, from Halloween costumes to Christmas ornaments to Chinese takeout. We may hear a trustworthy Voice telling us that we were never soldiers to be commanded but always children to be loved.

This is the same inner voice that calls to us, *Go where the life is. Even if it takes you away from what you've been taught. Even if it sounds like heresy to your indoctrinated mind, go with what feels true in your heart.*

THE NO-OWE INVITATION

Do Free Writing

This is a powerful exercise anytime, but particularly so in times of intense emotion. (I've encountered variations of this tool in several places; it's similar to Morning Pages in Julia Cameron's *The Artist's Way*, and the staff at The Clearing also teach a form of this process.)

The exercise is simple: Get a pen and a pile of blank paper. Set a timer and write for fifteen minutes. During this time, keep your hand moving continually; write anything and everything that comes up for you. Nothing is off-limits; as long as your hand is moving and you're writing, you're doing the exercise correctly. Let everything out onto the page; hold nothing back. Say exactly what you think and how you feel. Tell the truth of your own experience. Write what is real for you, here, now, today.

When your time is up, do not reread your words. Instead, destroy the paper completely. Personally, I love to burn the paper, but since I'm often in places where it's not safe to do so, I'll soak the paper in water and then tear up the sodden pieces. Knowing that I will destroy the paper as soon as I'm done writing gives me a sense of freedom to be real and raw. Try it and see what happens when you give yourself the gift of this releasing.

3

You Don't Owe Anyone
a Savior

Do you mind even a little that you are still addicted to
people-pleasing, and are still putting everyone else's needs
and laundry and career ahead of your creative, spiritual life?
Giving all your life force away, to "help" and impress. Well,
your help is not helpful, and falls short.
> —Anne Lamott, Facebook, May 2014

HERE'S WHAT I KNOW about you, dear one: You do a lot. You work hard. You are not lazy—no, heaven forbid. You make a list of things to do each day, and even though it's far too ambitious, you march through it like a good soldier.

You genuinely enjoy some of the things on that list. Some of them really matter to you, especially the ones that involve helping other people. (Maybe not doing their laundry, though.) When asked, you'd say yes, of course you want to lead that volunteer effort, call your friend in crisis, and send that thoughtful gift. Though to be precise, the truth is that you *would* want to do those things if you weren't so tired. Your secret is that you're very tired. And your depletion is less about the number of tasks on your list and more about how you carry them. The drain comes from believing that it all depends on you.

The energetic demand of saving the world is astronomical.

But since you think that you owe the world a savior, you keep going. You keep showing up and doing those good, helpful, kind things for others even when you're spent. It does not cut both ways, though. You do not consistently do good, helpful, kind things *for yourself* when you're exhausted. There's always more saving work to do on behalf of others, so your own restorative time gets the shaft. Secretly, you long for simple pleasures such as taking a nap when you're tired, burying your head in a book, or sipping a cup of tea slowly while staring out the window. But these activities feel too costly. You're in debt, after all! You don't have time to be lazy! You owe the world a savior!

If you've just now acknowledged that there's an issue and are already feeling stressed about how to fix it, remember this: You get to take the pressure off. Even for a moment, just let the awareness be enough. Just let yourself see what you see and feel what you feel. Let yourself notice that you've been driving too hard and too fast, trying to fix, save, and manage everything.

By giving yourself just a little space, you've already taken a powerful step forward, even if it doesn't feel like it.

As I shared earlier, when you've been speeding through life in savior mode for a long time, there's a kind of comfort in the stress. It's what you know. It's draining, but it also feels safe in some fundamental way. Plus, it's also a power trip, and it's sort of thrilling. *How fast can I go without crashing? How far can I go on fumes?*

But what would your life look like if you knew how to slow down and even just stop sometimes? What if you had permission to go at an unhurried pace? What if you didn't have to swoop in and save the world? What if the only life you could save was your own?

AS YOU PREPARE to shift out of trying to save others, it helps to understand what got you so revved up in the first place.

To this end, let's look at family systems theory. In this theory, created by Dr. Murray Bowen, the family is an interconnected and interdependent emotional unit. To oversimplify a little bit, Bowen theorized that when one person in the family changes, everyone else must change too, at least to some degree. When one person gets upset, the others feel it too. Over time, the fear, anxiety, and stress become collective.

When this happens, typically there are one or two people in the family unit who "take point" and take on the emotional responsibility.

"These are the people who accommodate the most to reduce tension in others," the Bowen Center website notes. "It is a reciprocal interaction. For example, a person takes too much responsibility for the distress of others in relationship to their unrealistic expectations of him, or a person gives up too much control of his thinking and decision-making in relationship to others anxiously telling him what to do. The one who does the most accommodating literally 'absorbs' system anxiety and thus is the family member most vulnerable to problems such as depression, alcoholism, affairs, or physical illness."

This accommodation is dangerous, yet it can be tough to spot because the ways that people accommodate vary. For example, some children hide their fear or sadness behind high-achieving, overly responsible, and perfectionistic behavior. In other theories of family dysfunction, such individuals are referred to as "The Family Hero" or "The Golden Child." (In case it's not wildly obvious, this is how I identify.)

Other children respond to the same family anxiety by rebelling and acting out ("The Scapegoat"), dissociating and dreaming themselves away ("The Lost Child"), or joking around and people-pleasing ("The Mascot"). Whichever role they choose, these children are trying desperately to decrease the distress in their families. They're trying to fix, help, and save in their own way.

All of us have probably "tried on" each of these roles at some point in our lives. The trouble comes when we get stuck in one role and believe that it is our whole identity. In fact, one reliable way to discern the degree of relational dysfunction in a family is to ask, "How much freedom do members have to move between roles?" If it's not

OK for members to show up "out of character"—for the Golden Child to fail, for the Scapegoat to succeed—then chances are it's a highly dysfunctional system.

Growing up, did you ever feel that you'd been cast in a role early on and that you couldn't possibly break character?

—

"MOMMY, SINCE DADDY DOESN'T go to church with us, will he get to be with us in the World Tomorrow?"

It was past my eight-year-old bedtime, but I'd summoned up my courage and headed down the hall to talk to my mom because I needed an answer. Mom was sitting on her bed reading her big Life Application Study Bible, just as I'd guessed she would be.

After I asked, Mom leaned over and gave me a hug. I breathed in her scent, part face cream and part indefinable Mom.

She said, "Oh, Caroline, you don't need to worry about that. Here, I'll show you why." She flipped through the thin, white pages of her Bible and read aloud: "For the unbelieving husband has been sanctified through his wife, and the unbelieving wife has been sanctified through her believing husband. Otherwise your children would be unclean, but as it is, they are holy."

She concluded, "So of course we all want Dad to come to church, but you don't need to worry that he won't be saved if he doesn't, OK?"

"Oh, OK," I said, running my fingers over the bedspread instead of twirling my hair. Mom had told me to stop my nervous habit, and I was doing my best. "Thanks, Mom. Good night."

"Good night, sweetie! I love you, Cari. My favorite daughter."

"I love you too, my favorite mother."

Mom's words came as a relief—sort of—but they also opened up new questions. Questions I never went back to ask. (That's not what Golden Children do; they're supposed to get it right the first time.)

If Dad was saved because of Mom, then why was Dad the bottom line in our house? On the rare days when I dared to argue with Mom, Dad would call me into his office to discuss the situation in a serious voice. He'd ask me to explain what I'd done wrong and why. I could practically see the cartoon thought bubble above his head: *A good father makes sure that his children know right from wrong.* The lecture style might have worked with a more rebellious child, but by the time I reached Dad's office to talk about whatever I'd done wrong that day, I already felt awful about myself. Since I staggered under the weight of my own shame, I couldn't bear the addition of Dad's disappointment. Those talks made me want to run away, just like Willie did.

And if we were saved because of Mom, had our whole family been unclean before, when no one went to church? Had Mom tried so hard to keep every commandment and observe every Feast in order to save us? If so, how could she ever really rest?

This version of faith was akin to the game Perfection, a race to fit all of the pieces into their proper slots. In Perfection, faltering or letting a hand slip meant running out of time. Then the board would pop up, the explosion of pieces a clear indictment: *Not quick enough. Not smart enough. Not good enough.* I was so busy trying not to fail that I rarely paused to question whether it was a game worth playing.

OUR MOST PREVAILING INTERNAL metaphors have a way of showing up in the physical world. If you have "not good enough" playing on repeat in your mind, then it won't be long before you start to believe that you're broken. Right around the time that Perfection picked up steam in my life, I broke my arm. During my third grade year, I was racing around the front yard with a friend, both of us chasing Curley. It was great fun, right up until we fell onto the grass and my friend's knee landed on my arm. I felt one of my left forearm bones snap; I felt a bolt of pain and fear.

As I gasped and struggled to get up off the lawn, the first words out of my mouth were, "I broke it."

Mom rushed over. "Oh, honey, I'm sorry you fell. But your arm looks fine! Why would you think that?"

All I could say was "I felt it break. It's broken."

"Broken? No!" Mom said, tilting her head. "I *saw* you. It was just a little tumble, for goodness' sake. Maybe you sprained it, but I doubt it. Let's just get you some ice."

This moment brings us back to one of the biggest misconceptions about trauma. Many people think that only capital-*T* Trauma is legitimate. In this way of thinking, only a big, dramatic physical injury such as a broken arm counts as traumatic. But what I've come to understand is that little-*t* trauma counts too. Being told by a trusted parent that you didn't break your arm is a different kind of pain, but it's no less real. Little-*t* trauma tends to come in quiet moments, in times when we get the message that it's not safe to know what we know or feel what we feel. The danger of this kind of trauma doesn't come from just one moment or one single incident; it's a slower, more subtle erosion of trust and confidence. Little-*t* trauma isn't a broken bone; it's a series of small cuts that slowly drain the life out of you.

Psychologist and author Dr. Valerie Rein defines trauma this way: "Trauma is any experience that made you feel unsafe in your fullest authentic expression and led to developing trauma adaptations to keep you safe."

How does it feel to think about your life through the lens of this broader definition of trauma? Are you starting to see the moments where you made excuses and brushed aside real pain?

For example, did you ever tell your truth only to have an authority figure deny it immediately and emphatically? Did a trusted adult ever negate your reality?

If so, then you know how quickly your mind tries to resolve the cognitive dissonance. *They must be right*, you reason, *so I must be wrong.*

When I broke my arm and my mom told me that I hadn't, her words made me doubt what I'd known just a moment ago. Right away, I started seeing the situation differently. My arm did look fine, even if it hurt. Maybe how it looked was more important than how it felt. Plus I had a dance recital coming up, and a clunky cast would clash with the costumes. So I did my best to believe that it wasn't broken.

Mom helped me ice my arm. "This will help. And if it still hurts, we can take you to see the doctor after school tomorrow. It'll be OK."

"But…" I said, then stopped. I left the rest of the sentence unspoken: *It really hurts now.* The Worldwide Church of God didn't encourage its members to see doctors when they were sick. Instead, church leadership anointed people with oil and prayed over them. Every year, I handed my teachers paperwork given to me from my mom, detailing my religious exemption from standard vaccinations. In this context, Mom's mention of going to the doctor was a big deal. I didn't push the issue.

The next day, Mom wrapped my arm to support it and sent me off to school. But since I wrote with my left hand, it was a struggle to hold a pencil and complete my worksheets. When Mom picked me up in the afternoon, I said what had been true all along, "I'm sorry, Mom, but it just really hurts."

"It does?" she asked, frowning. "OK then, I guess we'll go to the doctor," she said, resigned.

At urgent care, she confided in the nurse, "My daughter had a fall yesterday, and she thinks she broke her arm. It wasn't a hard fall. So we're just here to get it checked out."

The nurse nodded and handed me off to the tech for X-rays, a short, dull buzz, and then a long wait. At last, the doctor brought the films into the exam room and clipped them to the screen on the wall. "Well, it's definitely broken," the doctor said, almost cheerfully. "Looks like you were right, little lady. Time to get you into a cast."

I sucked in a breath, thinking, *I knew it! It really happened.*

"Oh! Oh! But I saw her fall … it didn't look bad!" Mom spoke, haltingly.

"It's OK, Mom," I said. "Like you said, it didn't look broken. It's just that I felt it."

If you were a savior-child yourself, then you know that in speaking those words, I was living by the primary rule: parents must not be made to feel bad, ever. Even when you were wounded by their action or inaction, you minimized the issue instinctively. You took it upon yourself to save them from the pain of true things.

AS CHILDREN, WE DON'T always know what to do with those truths we pushed aside in order to protect our parents. The pain lives within us until we find a way to let it out.

Art is the medium through which our unspoken truths reveal themselves. This is why therapists who help young children heal from trauma encourage them to draw or paint how they're feeling. This is why so many of us have healed parts of ourselves through dancing or singing. When age or terror limits our vocabulary, art gives us a new way to speak.

And it doesn't even have to be our own art. Sometimes when we're uncovering past trauma and struggling through present pain, we need another artist to help us. We need to hear from another person who has been to the depths, another person who has suffered and survived.

Jeannette Winterson said it well: "All of us, when in deep trauma, find we hesitate, we stammer; there are long pauses in our speech. The thing is stuck. We get our language back through the language of others. We can turn to the poem. We can open the book. Somebody has been there for us and deep-dived the words."

So if there's something you cannot speak about, something that is stuck within you, see how it feels to dive into the art of someone who has been where you are. Then, when you're ready, make your own art.

I'll offer just one point of caution: Do not share your art with those who catalyzed the trauma in the first place. At least, not right away. I'm not saying don't ever publish or share it—goodness knows I wouldn't be writing this book otherwise—but keep it private until you're prepared to face pushback. I learned that lesson the hard way.

MONTHS LATER, MY BROKEN arm had healed and my cast was long gone. As was my after-school custom, I was curled up on the armchair reading while Mom rifled through my school papers.

"Caroline, come here, please," she said, breaking my concentration. Her voice was too tight, too contained. I sucked in a breath, scanning my mind for infractions. No trespasses sprang to mind. I walked to the kitchen, where Mom stood at the counter holding up a writing assignment. "What does this say?" she asked, jabbing her finger at one sentence and wrinkling the paper. "Read it."

"'I broke my left arm,'" I read. "After three days, my parents took me to the doctor for a cast.'" I looked up at her, puzzled and uncomprehending.

Her cheeks were flushed and her eyes were fiery. "What were you *thinking*? Caroline! This is not true." Mom's words weren't quite as loud as a shout, but I felt the anger in them. "It was less than twenty-four hours between when you fell and when we took you to the doctor!" she cried. "How could you say that? Do you want your teacher to think that we don't take care of you?"

This response was shocking to me. I'd been expecting the usual praise for good grades, not a series of questions for which there was no possible answer. I hadn't meant any harm by the essay; I'd just gotten into the flow of the assignment and wrote what felt true for me.

Frantically, I searched my mind for an explanation. How had this mistake happened? From the WCG, I knew that three days was the length of time that God's people typically waited for deliverance. Jonah in the whale, Christ in the tomb—three days was the standard for ruin-to-rising. *I guess I got real life mixed up with the Bible*, I thought.

"I'm . . . I'm sorry, Mom. It was an accident. I got confused—"

She wasn't having it. "What is *wrong* with you? Did you do this *on purpose*?"

I froze. How could Mom believe I'd do that? I'd never even considered it. My hands gripped the back of a kitchen chair. On my last birthday, Mom had tied two balloons on that chair, and she'd baked my favorite vanilla cake with rainbow nonpareils so that I could celebrate with my friends. But in the face of Mom's fury, that happy time felt far away.

Mom raised her voice to a shout: "Do you want me and Daddy to get in trouble with the school or with the *police*? Do you want us to go to *jail*? Is that what you *want*?"

"No, Mommy," I said, so softly as to be barely audible. Panic rose in my chest like a bird; there was a frantic fluttering of wings, a confusion of feathers and fear.

"Just *go* to your *room!*" Mom shouted. "And leave your book with me." She sighed and shook her head with deep dismay. "Your brother, well, you know how much trouble he can get into! But *you*? I expect better from you."

Being sent to my room in exile felt like the end of the world, like the last days in Revelation that our pastor talked about in sermons.

WHEN SAVIOR-CHILDREN LIKE US face punishment, we blame ourselves. When our guardians send us away, we believe that we must be at fault. We have done the unforgivable; we have not kept to the correct narrative. We have stepped out of our prescribed role; we have revealed truths that were not supposed to be spoken or written.

And yet, what else could we have done? To quote Jeanette Winterson, "I needed words because unhappy families are conspiracies of silence. The one who breaks the silence is never forgiven. He or she has to learn to forgive him or herself."

At the time my mom yelled at me for writing that essay, I didn't know how to forgive myself. I didn't know how to give myself grace for breaking the silence, for telling the experiential (if not factual) truth about the day I broke my arm.

Since I didn't know about self-forgiveness, I felt stuck and scared. My mind ping-ponged desperately, trying to come up with rules to prevent this punishment from happening again. First, I went back to basics: *Mistakes mean I am unlovable, so I cannot make them. I just have to be perfect.* But then I thought, *It's all my fault. I can't remember things right. The way I remember is wrong and bad. I cannot trust myself.*

This is the double bind that we face as children, the one that we carry into adulthood: *Be perfect, but never forget that you're broken.*

THE FIRST PART OF getting free from the savior complex is actually letting ourselves feel the pain of living this way. The point here is not to add any unnecessary pain but rather to give ourselves permission to access the underlying pain that is already present.

This is about awareness, not another rush to fix a perceived problem. When we want to make significant changes, we need time to tune into what's really going on in our lives. We need to take a closer look, to notice when we're trying to fix, save, or rescue others. It may be subtle. For example, we may be psychologically tiptoeing around certain people, trying to manage their emotional reactions and prevent them from getting upset. Or we may be showing up or staying in touch because we're afraid of what would happen if we let go of the relationship.

When the impulse to interfere in another person's life arises, we can ask ourselves, "What's really going on here? What am I avoiding in my own life by meddling in theirs?"

Typically, we're working hard to avoid a repeat of a painful experience from our past. We don't want others to be mad or disappointed because then we'll feel that same old shame, and it will be awful! If that's the case, we must give ourselves permission to go gently, feel a little bit at a time, and practice applying love to the parts of us that hurt. This is emotional first aid; this cleans the toxins out of the wounds and sets us up to heal.

In this process, we resist the conditioned impulse to brush off past hurts and pretend that they were no big deal. Minimizing our hurts without tending to them is like deciding not to sanitize a cut because it's "just a scratch." What starts off as a minor wound may get infected and lead to big problems.

I can say that with confidence because when I was ten years old, I witnessed the WCG's leadership attempt to sidestep decades of its members' emotional pain. I saw some truly epic spiritual bypassing; I saw botched, surface-level attempts to heal deep hurts.

In early 1995, the WCG was going through what grown-ups called "the changes." To sum up, the head honchos decided that we were a New Covenant church, no longer under the Old Covenant legalism. This meant that all of those highly specific religious rules we'd worked so hard to keep for years were officially out the window; from now on, the WCG was going to be more like mainstream Christian churches. We'd have more talk about Jesus and less talk about the evils of Christmas. The pastor general recorded a sermon that was angry and schismatic, with no acknowledgment that this change was traumatic for many. Rather, the subtext of the message was that we should simply skip over our pesky hurt feelings and just be glad to be free from the old legalism. (And of course, we should not question the authorities who had made this decision!) More pastors responded with more yelling. I remember listening and thinking, *How about all of the pastors agree to stop yelling? That would be a great New Covenant rule.* When the church splintered, people left in droves. This makes perfect sense to me now, but at the time, my friends and I just wondered, *Why are all of the grown-ups so tense?*

After the church split, there were fewer girls my age around, and those of us who remained banded together. The year we turned thirteen, my friends Tam, Eva, Mandy, and I all started calling each other *best friends*, a term that thrilled me. We were gawky teenagers from New Jersey with ill-advised bangs, braces, and Limited Too T-shirts, but we thought of ourselves as quite mature because we flew overseas to church camp together in Scotland. Our old friend Marie met us at a London bus station parking lot, pointing out people she knew from camp the year before.

"Wait until you meet the guys in the camp band! I swear, you'll just die, they are so fine. Wait, sorry, I take back the swear. Sorry, God!" She raised her eyes skyward for a moment. Using the word *swear* or swearing an oath was considered sinful in our church.

"I didn't mean to swear . . . oh, there's Tom," she said, gesturing to a guy standing with another group. "He's older than me—fifteen or sixteen, maybe? Anyway, he's so funny. But he's also kind of *wild.*" Marie dropped her voice on the last word.

At thirteen, I thought that Tom looked both grown-up and intensely alive. Standing there in that unromantic parking lot with bus fumes filling the air, I felt a flicker of something like longing.

I wasn't looking for a boyfriend, though, and the first time I fell in love, it was with the camp itself. With the exception of the biting clouds of midges, I loved everything about it. I loved walking across the dewy green field to breakfast in the morning and singing at the top of my lungs at sing-a-longs at night. I loved hearing all the different accents and unfamiliar expressions such as "Brilliant" and "Well done!" I loved being a foreigner in a predominantly British crowd and how this made me something close to cool for the first time in my life. I loved standing on the shores of Loch Lomond and feeling deeply connected to this place I'd never been before.

As luck or fate would have it, my dorm and Tom's were paired up as brother-and-sister dorms, and soon we got to talking. He asked me to go with him to the formal dining banquet at the end of camp, and of course I said yes.

The next year at camp, we spent much of our free time together on the beach, laughing and skipping rocks across the water. We weren't exactly alone, though; staff members patrolled the area to make sure that campers weren't "canoodling." One Saturday morning when Tom had brought his guitar out to play for me, a staffer approached us and said, "You two, can you put a bit more distance between you?"

Immediately I shifted several feet, but Tom didn't budge. He stopped playing Deep Blue Something's "Breakfast at Tiffany's," but he kept his hands on the metal guitar strings and said, "Why? We're not doing anything wrong."

The staffer muttered, "I'm just saying, keep a bit more distance, all right?"

Furiously embarrassed, I could hardly look at Tom. At that point, we hadn't so much as held hands. But Tom didn't seem embarrassed at all. "Can't believe that. He's got nothing better to do than bother us?"

"Guess not," I said, my voice low. When he said it, *Us* sounded like a lion: fierce, beautiful, not to be trifled with. I loved it and I was scared by it in equal measure.

With the help of our friends ferrying feelings back and forth, Tom and I began a long-distance relationship. We didn't have Skype or even email, so we hand-wrote letters and spoke on the phone once a week.

Mom was decidedly unenthusiastic about me being in a romantic relationship, though, or even watching one play out on TV. If we were watching a show and couples kissed passionately (or worse yet, headed for a bedroom), she'd turn away from the screen and say, "Ugh! Seriously, that's enough!"

I'd wince and plead, "Mom, please . . . can you not do that? Can't we just watch the show?" Then we'd lapse into silence. If tensions were running particularly high, she'd say, "Caroline, this is my house and my television, and I can say whatever I want. Would you rather not watch this show at all?"

Perhaps she was doing her best to deter me from sex, and if so, her strategy worked. I couldn't wait for my first real kiss, but I also had a lot of apprehension about it. I associated kissing with that TV-time grimace, the dreaded turning away of approval. But the balance of my life was changing; I was starting to care more about seeing Tom than being the Golden Child.

My parents sensed this shift. When I begged them to allow Tom to visit, Mom's was the deciding vote: *No*. She wouldn't allow Tom to stay in our home or even allow me to see him if he stayed at a friend's home in the United States. Considering that I was allowed to see him at camp with zero parental supervision, this seemed unreasonable. I'd been sent to my room very few times in my life, usually in an agony of guilt. But after that argument, I went willingly, stomping up the stairs and slamming the door behind me.

FOR THOSE OF US who felt like we had to be "good" and thereby save our parents, siblings, or peers, the teen years were fraught. We tried to individuate and create distance, but we weren't used to conflict and disapproval. We wanted our parents or guardians to offer love instead of rules and restrictions, but often the changes in us prompted them to double down on control. Perhaps they wanted to keep us close, but the sad truth is that control only pushed us further away. So instead we turned to other relationships for safety.

Tom's missives kept coming in the mail, and I listened to the mixtape he gave me every night. But Tom wasn't the only one to whom

I was devoted. At fifteen, I'd started taking my faith more seriously. Since I'd spent childhood hearing almost exclusively about a God of judgment, the more compassionate Jesus figure was tremendously appealing. I read the New Testament in earnest, along with Robin Jones Gunn's Christy Miller novels. The latter featured a sweet, super-Christian heroine, her cute surfer boyfriend, and their posse of pals, all of whom believed the same things about God with the same degree of certainty. Christy and her friends had purity pledges, missions trips, and oceanic baptisms, and I was so inspired that I decided to be baptized too. On July 16, 2000, my parents and brother gathered with Eva, Tam, Mandy, and their family members to witness the immersion.

Soon I was showered with congratulatory cards, words of encouragement, and a "spiritual birthday" cake. The fact that I'd been dunked in the associate pastor's small basement pool rather than the vast ocean like Christy Miller did not matter to me. What mattered was that I had promised to follow Love wherever it led.

WHEN I TOLD TOM about the baptism between kisses at camp that year, he said that he was happy I was happy. But that wasn't enough for me. I had to tell him why Jesus was so compelling for me and how amazing it was to feel like God actually cared.

Tom and I kept up our letters and calls after camp, but by autumn, something shifted. My letters were earnest, preachy, and not-so-subtly focused on "saving" him. According to my new belief system, this was only right; I was a sinner, but I was also supposed to save other people. This sort of theology swings from shame to self-aggrandizement and back again. One moment you're a lowly sinner, and the next—look! You're a spiritual hero who knows what's best for others before they do!

And if this wasn't off-putting enough, Tom was far more disillusioned with the WCG than I'd realized. He'd started stepping away from the New Covenant church just as I'd been swept up into it, and the God question drove a wedge between us. Those Deep Blue Something lyrics Tom had sung for me on the beach started to ring eerily true: The world had come between us. Our lives had come between us.

Yet the catalyst for our breakup was both simpler and more cliché: Tom got drunk at a party and kissed another girl. At least, that was the story I heard. Tom called me the day after, and while he was clearly upset about something, he chose not to tell me what had happened. He left that responsibility to the social grapevine. When my friends told me the real story at church the next week, I was a basket case.

On the drive home, my mom tried to comfort me as I sobbed in the passenger seat.

"Cari, it's OK," she said, soothingly.

"It. Is. Not. OK!" My breath came in little gasps; I had to try hard not to hyperventilate. How could it be OK when Tom didn't love me anymore and probably never had?

But then I remembered the pile of pale-blue airmail envelopes he had sent over the last two years and all the time we'd spent on the phone, every minute an expense. That was the worst of it, really—not that we hadn't loved each other, but that we had. We'd just made different choices. I'd tried to cram my religion down his throat, and he'd crammed his tongue down someone else's.

"Oh, honey, I'm sorry about this," Mom broke into my thoughts.

She was trying to be there for me, I knew. But grief and anger knotted in my chest, and my voice came out bitter and sarcastic: "Wasn't this what you wanted? Tom's definitely not coming to visit now! You didn't like him, and now he's gone! Hooray!"

She tried to console me, but I was inconsolable.

"Caroline, honey," Mom said. "Please, calm down. It's OK. It'll be OK. God will help you heal from this. He makes all things work together for the good of those that love Him, remember?"

I could not think of a worse time for Bible verses. I broke my silence just long enough to say, "Please. Stop."

She did. We rode home in silence.

THE SEVERE MERCY OF the breakup was that it shattered my illusion of control. For a long time, I stopped trying to save anybody else. I had to; it took all of my energy and focus just to get through each day without breaking down.

If you've ever been heartbroken, then you may know how tempting it is to pretend that you're not in so much pain. Our culture tells us that when bad things happen, we are allowed to feel upset for about a day, then we're supposed to Get Over It. But our emotions do not move at the same speed as our thoughts; emotional processing takes more time than mental processing does.

We can avoid our sadness, anger, and grief; we can push them down for a while. But emotions have a natural buoyancy. You've heard the expression *Truth always rises to the surface*? Emotions are like that too. John Green summed it up in *The Fault in Our Stars*: "That's the thing about pain, it demands to be felt."

That's what I learned the next summer at camp. That year I was assigned the same dorm as my close friend Tam, but unfortunately, our dorm leader just so happened to be Tom's new girlfriend, the same girl he'd kissed at the party. Even in that comically bad setup, though, I wouldn't let myself break down again. I pretended that I was fine, that it didn't bother me a bit.

I pushed down the fear and grief until one night Tam climbed down from her top bunk and scooted over onto my bottom bunk.

"Hey! What are you doing?" I whispered. "It's after lights-out!"

Even as I said it, I knew that we wouldn't get in trouble. This was the silver lining of having Tom's girlfriend as our dorm leader: Tam and I knew that we could talk after lights-out or skip dorm meetings with zero consequences.

Scooting closer, Tam whispered, "Cari, I can tell you're trying really hard to be strong about this breakup and being in this dorm and everything. But . . . I think you need to cry. In fact, I'm not leaving until you do."

"I don't need to . . ." But I couldn't finish the sentence because it wasn't true, and we both knew that.

"Yes, honey," Tam said, gently. "Yes, you do."

"Wow, this is awkward," I fumbled. "I don't know if I can cry. I haven't for a long time."

"That's OK. Just try, OK? And I'll be here." As she said that, she reached over and wrapped both her arm and a scratchy tartan blanket around my shoulder.

The kindness of that gesture loosened something in my heart.

Tam and I sat huddled together for a time in the quiet. I heard the faint sound of the loch lapping against the rocky shore. I sensed all of the other girls around us sleeping.

In that patient space, I finally let go. I wept for Tom, for the loss of the relationship. I wept because it was all so painful and because I was tired of pretending that it wasn't.

The invitation to fall apart was exactly what I'd been avoiding and exactly what I needed. By holding space for me to be heart-broken, Tam showed me that I was strong enough to feel my own pain. Rather than pointing me toward an external savior, she helped me connect to the vulnerable, wounded parts of myself. She didn't feel my pain for me; she felt it with me, and that made all the difference.

———

THE DAY AFTER TAM helped me cry, I was astonished to wake up feeling . . . *better.* It wasn't happiness, exactly, but I had an unexpected sense of strength and peace. I wasn't feeling that way because I'd seen Tom and we'd reconciled (although that did happen later). I was feeling better because I'd come back to *myself.*

For months, I'd been thinking, *If only he'd told me the truth,* or *If only he'd love me.* But freedom was only a pronoun away: If only *I'd* told myself the truth. If only *I'd* love me.

The old story in our psyches tells us that as long as we can get another person to love us and do what we want, then we'll be happy. But there's a wonderful phrase that Byron Katie uses: "Skip the middle-man, and be happy from here." In other words, nobody else needs to change in order for me to be happy. My happiness is 100 percent my responsibility.

Trying to save someone else is a crazy-making proposition, not only because it's above our pay grade, but because it distances us from the truth of our own hearts. The more we long to save others, the more we need to take a look at where we're struggling within ourselves. We tend to project our problems outward: if only I could fix and save this person, then everything would be fine! But the only life we can save is our own, and the only pain we can resolve is our own.

THE NO-OWE INVITATION

Work with Your Projections

Projection is a psychological term for how we tend to put our own issues and anxieties onto other people. We displace—or project—them onto others, or onto our concept of God, so that we don't have to deal with them for ourselves. The catchphrase "You spot it, you got it" applies here—often the thing that frustrates you most about another person is indicative of a part of yourself that you haven't fully accepted yet.

We all do this, so the objective of this exercise is not to beat yourself up for projecting! Rather, the idea is to become aware of your projections and use them as valuable information to help guide your life going forward.

First, find your projections by making a list of how you judge someone else, or God: "I judge this person as [fill in the blank]." Be honest here; do not sugarcoat. Write what you really think— write the truth that you don't want to admit to anyone!

If you're having trouble judging on paper, Byron Katie's Judge Your Neighbor worksheet is a great resource. (It's available for free online at her website, TheWork.com.)

Here's an example of how the judge-on-paper process works. Say that you're mad at your friend Monica because you believe that she wastes your time by showing up late to your coffee dates. So you write, "I judge Monica as a total time-waster."

Then, take a deep breath, ground yourself in loving energy, and take a look at how those judgments apply to you. Take one judgment at a time and work it through this script. (I learned this process from the counseling team at The Clearing, and they learned it from Drs. Ron and Mary Hulnick through their Spiritual Psychology program at the University of Santa Monica.) You might even want to speak each judgment aloud.

"I judge [person] as [judgment]. I can now see and accept that I can be [judgment], and that is OK." (Pause and take a look at how that's true in your relationship with yourself, others, and/or God as you understand God.) "My intention going forward is [set a positive intention from your loving heart space]."

Here's one example of how it could look:

I judge Monica as a total time-waster. I can now see and accept that I can be a total time-waster, and that is OK. (Do I spend my own time in ways that feel like a waste? If I'm waiting around for Monica when I know that she's always late, who is really wasting my time? Is it her, or is it me?) My intention going forward is to spend my time wisely, in a way that aligns with my values. My intention going forward is to set a boundary on the amount of time I spend waiting for Monica. My intention is to honor my own time.

This might sting a bit at first—the ego does not love noticing where it's been hypocritical!—but if you stay with it, it's tremendously freeing. You thought that if you could just get someone else to change, then you'd be happy. But that was you giving your power away. This exercise helps you get your power back.

4

You Don't Owe Anyone

a Brave Face

I always put on a brave face when I was the most terrified,
the most trapped and out of control.
—Natalia Kills, "I Thought I Would Be Dead by Now"

DID YOU READ THE Little House books when you were young?
I did. Back then, Laura Ingalls was my hero. Though my family lived
in suburban New Jersey, I created a "claim shanty" in our backyard in
true pioneer spirit. My grandmother made me a sunbonnet, which
I tied proudly under my chin. I told my younger cousins all about
how Laura and her family prepared for winter on the Dakota plains.
Together we piled logs (read: twigs) to build fires and ward off the
cold. We had no real concept of a subzero winter in an uninsulated
space. Like so many children before us, we fell in love with a romanti-
cized version of Laura's life.

As an adult, I went back and read the Little House books again,
and they sounded very different. There was the spirit of adventure,
yes, and there was also serious anti-indigenous racism. There was
fiddling and dancing, but there was also terrible deprivation and

uncertainty. *The Long Winter* wasn't romantic—it was horrifying. The whole town nearly died of exposure or starvation or both.

Why am I telling you this? There comes a time in every life when metaphorical blizzards arise, when storm clouds block the light and strong winds howl. One minute you're looking at clear skies; the next, you're surrounded by a blinding fury. It isn't your fault, and it certainly isn't within your control. If that's what your life is like right now, I'm so sorry that this is happening to you. I know that you feel shocked and afraid, that everything—from breathing to brushing your teeth—is ten times harder than usual.

How do you survive in a literal or metaphorical blizzard? Find the nearest shelter, the closest safe place. Once there, keep warm and stay hydrated. Ask for help and supplies. Go into survival mode and let nonessentials go. Do not allow harsh self-talk and cold judgment to chill you further. When you're already freezing, that's the most dangerous thing you can do. Instead, practice being kind to yourself. Talk to yourself as you would a beloved child. Congratulate yourself on the most basic self-nurturing decisions. (You went back to bed when you felt tired? Fantastic. You made yourself a cup of tea and wrapped yourself in a blanket? Brilliant.) In the context of your ordinary life, it's easy to take such tasks for granted. But you are not in ordinary life any longer. You are in a blizzard. Here surviving is succeeding.

Most of all, don't waste your precious energy pretending that everything's fine, just fine! Do not buy into the belief that you owe anyone a brave face. This pretending is too costly for you. It's an energetic debt you can't afford to rack up.

That said, most of us have a deep culturally approved belief that we must "be strong and brave" in the face of adversity. If we're in a blizzard right now, it's likely that well-meaning people are telling us, "You'll be stronger for this!" "What doesn't kill you makes you stronger!"

In order to appease them, we put on a brave face before we feel ready, before we've even fully felt the extent of the damage.

A brave face is beautiful when it's honest. But when that brave face is a lie, when it's premature, that's when it hurts you. That's when it disconnects you from the truth of your experience.

One dictionary says that brave is about "showing no fear of dangerous or difficult things." But I prefer Glennon Doyle's definition, from *Untamed*: "Brave means living from the inside out. Brave means, in every uncertain moment, turning inward, feeling for the Knowing, and speaking it out loud. Since the Knowing is specific, personal, and ever changing, so is brave. Whether you are brave or not cannot be judged by people on the outside. Sometimes being brave requires letting the crowd think you're a coward. Sometimes being brave means letting everyone down but yourself."

That's what I mean by "You don't owe anyone a brave face." You don't owe anyone their version of brave. Your only job is to live according to your own Knowing. Sometimes other people will think that that looks brave, and sometimes they won't. It doesn't matter. *Bravery*, like *trauma*, is subjective. You know yourself best. You know when you're being brave, even if it seems humble and quiet from the outside.

When you're accustomed to binary thinking and duality, you see strength and weakness on opposite ends of the spectrum. But when you step into mystery and paradox, you realize that it's possible to hold both strength and weakness in the same moment. You might think, *I don't feel strong, so what's wrong with me?* But there's nothing wrong with you. It's just that strength doesn't always look and feel like you think it will.

When I was younger, I could quote the relevant Bible verse—"For when I am weak, then I am strong"—but I wasn't really *enrolled* in the idea. I thought that when I felt weak, it must mean that I wasn't strong. Surely having real strength meant that I wouldn't feel quite so vulnerable? I saw myself through that same old pair of shame glasses: never good enough, strong enough, or brave enough. But then in a counseling session in my twenties, I told a terrible story to my counselor. It was my own Long Winter, scary to talk about and scarier to live through. At the end of our session, she said, "You're so strong."

I was incredulous: "But I feel so weak."

She didn't miss a beat: "That's how it works."

That statement felt like a revelation. If I felt weak, I wasn't doing anything wrong? Feeling weak didn't disqualify me from being strong and brave? What a relief!

For recovering perfectionists and people-pleasers, it takes real strength to admit weakness. For us, bravery looks like dropping the brave face. Bravery looks like letting our true face—weeping, mourning, raging—show through. As we do, we discover a light within us that will outlast the wind and snow and cold.

When I was in high school, though, I didn't realize that. When a blizzard descended on my brother Willie and the rest of our family, I put on a brave face. And the more I hid my fear away, the colder I became.

WITH MY HIGH-SCHOOL MATH textbook open before me, I hummed along to the dc Talk song "What If I Stumble?" and rued the day I'd decided to enroll in advanced precalculus. My bedroom door was closed and locked, but I knew that Mom was downstairs chopping vegetables for supper, Willie was watching a video, and Dad was still at work.

Though I concentrated on the task at hand, a small section of my consciousness remained separate, listening. Over the last few months, this divided awareness had become my normal. While part of me was reading or writing or watching TV, another part was on alert, listening for a disturbance. The sense of normalcy I'd taken for granted had become terribly fragile. As Jodi Picoult wrote, "Normal, in our house, is like a blanket too short for a bed—sometimes it covers you just fine, and other times it leaves you cold and shaking; and worst of all, you never know which of the two it's going to be."

Willie was having severe behavioral issues, which was a polite way of saying that he flew into aggressive, self-injurious rages without warning. Was it a testosterone imbalance triggered by puberty? Was there a strong psychological component? We didn't know for sure, but our parents tried to minimize possible triggers: schedule changes, loud noises, overstimulation, and foods containing gluten or lactose. Most days Mom was on the phone with doctors, working to figure out why Willie had lost his mind. Some psychotropic drugs left Willie lethargic and vacant, while others made his behavior more dangerous than ever.

Willie had been expelled from our local public high school, and our parents hadn't found another school that would accept him. While they searched for a placement and took care of him around the clock, I tried even harder to be their bright shining star of a daughter, never causing them stress and needing as little as possible.

With that in mind, I refocused my mind on math problems and twirled my hair, just as I'd done back in grade school. From downstairs, I heard the opening notes of the Michael W. Smith song "Above All" cranked at top volume, and fear shot through my body. Sometimes Willie's meltdowns caught me unaware, but more often than not I'd sense a blizzard building.

The song volume went down, then back up again; I heard Mom telling Willie to turn it down. But as the song careened into its dramatic chorus, I heard a bang and a string of Willie's vocalizations. They were agitated and keening, furious and sad: "Eh-ohhh. Nehhhh. Eh-ohhh."

A loud crash followed. Racing to the top of the stairs, I stood still, listening. Mom and Dad had told me to let them handle things with Willie. But the truth was that when Dad wasn't home, Mom needed hands-on help to prevent Willie from injuring himself and her.

"Willie, how about you take ten deep breaths?" I heard Mom say.

Willie's breaths were so loud, I could hear them from the second-floor landing. "One," he rasped, then, "Two." "Three."

"Good job, Willie," Mom said. But midway through breath number four, Willie snapped.

"Eeeeeee-agghhh!" he shrieked. *We're screwed*, I thought.

I dashed downstairs and swung through the dining room, taking the quickest route to the kitchen, where Mom and Willie were facing off.

As my eyes swept the room, I noted the chef's knife sitting out on the cutting board amid a pile of cucumber slices. Willie had never cut anyone with a knife, but I was always afraid that he'd pick one up during a meltdown.

"Now, is this calm behavior?" Mom asked.

Willie bent his head to spit on the floor, then shouted, "*I'll* take ten deep breaths!" His voice was hostile, his eyebrows furrowed behind his round, Harry-Potter-style glasses.

"Willie, it's time to roll up in the rug now."

"I'll roll up in the rug!" he proclaimed at top volume.

But he didn't. Instead he mumbled in strange syllables, speaking a language I couldn't understand. Mom and I stood frozen, watching him. For a moment, we were suspended, the three of us under the same spell. Then Willie lunged forward to pick up a water glass from the counter.

Mom blinked and started toward him. "Willie, no, do *not*—"

Willie smashed the glass to the tile floor, and it shattered at our feet.

"Go roll up in the rug *right now!*" Willie obeyed, turning and running toward the living room. We followed him, backtracking to avoid the shards of broken glass. Willie wrapped himself up into the oriental rug once, twice, nearly three times. The rug was supposed to help protect him from himself, but he wrenched his neck out and bit his own shoulder. Jutting his head out, he banged it hard against the wood floor.

"Get your head into the rug!" Mom yelled. Willie did, but only after striking his skull once more. Mom and I snatched flowery sofa cushions and sat down on Willie's writhing body to provide calming pressure. Sometimes Willie surrendered to it and exuded relief right away, but this was not one of those times.

Intellectually, I understood that rolling up in the rug and applying pressure helped prevent the worst of Willie's self-injury. He'd given himself black eyes and severe bruises before; he was already his own worst enemy. Still, it felt terribly wrong to restrain him, to sit on top of my panicked brother. When I accidentally bit down on the tip of my tongue in the tousle, the blood in my mouth tasted like betrayal. Just for a moment, I relaxed my position atop his upper body. Willie took advantage, snaking out his right arm and clawing upward toward me. He scratched his fingernails hard against my forearm before Mom grabbed his arm and shoved it back into the rug.

"Ow! Stop it! Stop it! *God!*" I shrieked, smacking my palm down. I hit the rug, knowing that my brother would feel a muted strike against his back. I didn't care. The guilty thoughts were gone, replaced by furious anger.

Willie writhed and flailed for a few more minutes, but Mom and I managed to keep him contained in the rug. I heard his breathing start to slow, but my hands were in fists. My breathing was fast, and no matter how Willie whimpered, I didn't relax my hold or shift my weight. Later, when I was alone in the dark of my closet, I'd let myself sob and shake and hyperventilate. But until then, I'd put the feelings in a box and hide them away.

After a while, Willie started to weep, which I recognized as a sign that the danger had passed. The constant cycle of rage and regret was excruciating for him. When I imagined Willie's internal landscape, I saw the no man's land we learned about in history class, a bombed-out place between battles. My brother was trapped in a war between his biochemistry and his better self, victory always out of reach.

Yet when he said, "I'm sorry, Caroline," I couldn't summon a single word in response.

Mom turned to me, asking, "Are you all right? How's your arm?" She leaned over to look at the scratches.

"It'll be fine. You and Dad have worse." I viewed my own minor injuries from a great distance, as though they'd happened to someone else. More often Mom and Dad sported cuts, bruises, and bite marks from Willie, and the sight of them made my stomach clench.

"Make sure to put some antibacterial ointment on it, OK? I think your brother is calm now, so I'll go clean up the glass and finish up dinner."

"Yeah. I will," I said, but I stayed where I was, braced on top of my cushion and feeling it shudder in time with my brother's sobs. Though I shrugged my shoulders and feigned nonchalance, undertones of anger edged into my voice.

After Willie's rages, I felt brittle as kindling, ready to burst into flame. In the wake of another meltdown, I'd walked upstairs, picked up my brother's (admittedly flimsy) old guitar, and smashed it to pieces against his bed frame. It felt as though I'd lost control of my body. Was that what it was like to be Willie? What if I became like him?

After the guitar-smashing incident, I tried to keep a tighter lid on my emotions. I tried to be stronger. I tried to be what I thought was brave.

———

INCREASINGLY, THOUGH, I FOUND it hard to believe that anything in our house could get better. And losing hope made it hard to be around people who insisted upon maintaining it.

The night before, Mom had called me into her room, saying, "C'mon, Cari, let's say a prayer!" in an upbeat voice.

"Coming, Mom," I choked out. I trudged down the hallway to her and Dad's room, pausing in the doorway. I really didn't want to do our usual nightly prayer, but in our house, it wasn't optional.

Mom was sitting on the bed with her big study Bible open before her. She smiled and patted the comforter, and I took a seat.

She began, "Well, what should we pray about tonight? What do you think? Do you want to start?" But I didn't have faith in anything but the need for Willie to get into a mental hospital.

I'd begun pleading with Mom and Dad to get more intensive care for Willie, but the conversations went nowhere. Dad seemed somewhat open to the possibility of inpatient treatment, but at least in my presence, Mom refused to consider it. And so we stayed in the same awful limbo.

That was our reality. It felt unbearable, but maybe that was just because I was weak and sinful. *You need to be better*, the voice in my head reminded me. So I took a breath and did my best to smile at my mom. I didn't tell her how angry I was. Instead, I summoned up my brave face and answered with forced, deliberate calm, "You start the prayer, and I'll join in."

There was a rhythm to Mom's prayer, to the familiar words she spoke. And there was a rhythm to the waves of anger that washed over me, crashing in fury and receding in guilt: *I hate this, I'm sorry;*

I hate this, I'm sorry. Since I loved both my mom and God, I assumed that this rage was just my inherent sinfulness.

This brings us to one of the biggest problems with putting on the brave face. Maintaining this false face demands a specific kind of effort; it's all about reining in our "unacceptable" feelings. This process is predicated on the belief that the way we naturally feel in a given situation is wrong or bad. We're so focused on showing up "better" that we're distracted from the real issues.

We don't consider the radical possibility that we're not the problem. We don't see that often our anger is valid, that we're having a normal reaction to a dangerous situation.

When Mom finished her part of the prayer, she squeezed my hands, indicating that I should start. I did my best to say the right words.

After we said *Amen*, she gripped my hands again and beamed at me, pleased. "It's so good to pray together." She looked into my eyes as though expecting me to reply in the affirmative. But I was out of patience, and Mom's glad piety grated my last nerve. So when she held my gaze, I snapped, "*What?* What do you want me to say?"

Her reply was full of hurt: "Honey, why are you being like this?"

Good question, I thought. Why couldn't I just say something pleasant and innocuous—"Yes, it's so good for us to gather in prayer"? I knew that was what she wanted. The problem was, I wasn't good at lying outright. So I sighed and spoke a half-truth: "I'm just tired. So tired. Sorry I snapped. I really need to go to bed."

"OK, sweetie," she said. She leaned in to hug me, and I made myself hug her back.

TWENTY YEARS ON, WILLIE is still fighting the same battle. And so I have plenty of opportunities to practice putting away the old brave face.

Several years ago, when my parents and brother came to visit my husband Jonathan and me, Willie had a massive breakdown on a quiet, residential street. It was a perfect early-spring day, seventy degrees and sunny, all bright-green leaves and squirrels bounding and birds chirping. And then there was Willie, flinging himself to the ground, kicking trees, trying to strike our parents when they restrained him. I stood a few feet away and Jonathan stood with me, bearing witness.

If you've ever had a moment like that—if you've ever come face-to-face with the same scenario you feared for years—then you know how tempting it is to numb out and put on the same stifling brave face. In moments like those, standing with a safe person is a saving grace. When you have someone you trust beside you, you may find that you're able to stay present and breathe through the pain in a way you haven't before.

In her book *The Joy Diet*, Martha Beck quotes psychiatrist and trauma researcher Judith Herman: "While the unit of human physical survival is one, the unit of psychological survival is two. Without someone to connect with, we quite simply can't go on. Not any of us."

With Jonathan in my life, I feel physically and emotionally safer with my brother. Sometimes I risk leaning my head on Willie's shoulder, and he rests his head on top of mine. And sometimes when I pull away, he keeps his head bent toward me, as though he wants to stay close. And at other times I try to hug him gently, and he snaps his teeth at me.

At my wedding, he behaved beautifully, and I was so happy he could be there. But before my baby shower, he tried to punch our dad and hit his fists on the walls of my in-laws' house. I hid in a bedroom, wrapped my arms around my belly, and tried not to have an anxiety attack.

Now that I'm not in survival mode, I have more space to feel the full spectrum of feelings around my brother, from angry to awestruck and back again. In some ways, feeling more is horrible, but it's also the way forward. It's bringing me to a truer place, one that I couldn't access back when I was still wearing the old brave face.

Anne Lamott said it well in *Bird by Bird*: "It turns out that the truth, or reality is our home . . . But you can't get to any of these truths by sitting in a field smiling beatifically, avoiding your anger and damage and grief. Your anger and damage and grief are the way to the truth."

The brave face isn't the way to the truth. The way to the truth is through all of the things you thought you had to cover up *with* the brave face.

Loving someone who engages in highly dysfunctional behavior requires big-time bravery; it requires that you get really honest about what you can and cannot tolerate, what does and does not feel safe for you. For those of us who have witnessed and endured abuse, taking care of ourselves and setting boundaries can feel an awful lot like betrayal. And in a sense it is, because it means that we're questioning the old rules and shattering the story of self-sacrifice.

But sometimes we must break the rules so as not to betray ourselves any longer.

For years now I've maintained a boundary that I do not spend time alone with my brother without another physically capable adult present. This allows me to see Willie and be a part of his life without compromising my own safety. I also don't physically intervene when Willie melts down. I'll call for help or offer support in other ways, but I don't get in the middle anymore.

When I was younger, I thought those choices meant loving my brother less, so I didn't make them. But I don't believe that anymore. It's not about loving my brother less; it's about learning to love myself more.

THE NO-OWE INVITATION

Question Your Painful Thoughts, Judgments, and Limiting Beliefs

Most of us don't recognize how our thought patterns separate us from feeling peace. In the midst of loss and trauma, we put on a brave face while our minds, hearts, and spirits are subsumed by painful thoughts. Questioning those thoughts is an act of love.

First, identify a thought that is causing you pain. Don't sugarcoat the thought; be honest about exactly what you think and believe about a difficult situation. For example, perhaps in the past you might have said, "It's fine. I'll just get through it," but what you really think about it is, "This is horrible and hopeless," "I can't bear it," "It isn't fair," and, "It never should have happened this way."

Next, employ The Work of Byron Katie. The Work is a tool that helps you question those painful thoughts. It's a simple, powerful series of four questions and a turnaround. It's a type of meditation that shifts how you see the world. Following are the questions with my own responses, so you can see what The Work looks like in action.

Before I share it, though, I want to emphasize that The Work is definitely *not* about denying physical reality, excusing abuse, or ignoring neglect. Rather, it's about questioning painful thoughts so that you are clear, present, and prepared to love both yourself and others.

With that in mind, here's one personal example of The Work:

One of my most painful thoughts about Willie was *My brother is lost to me.* That belief gave rise to grief, fear, and anger whenever I bought into it.

The first question of The Work is "Is it true?"

 Is it true that my brother is lost to me, yes or no?

 Yes. (It feels true.)

 (For the first two questions, only answer yes or no. Don't go into elaborate stories or justifications; those will only take you off-track. Here I've added my thoughts in parentheses so you can see where the yes and no answers came from within me. There is no right or wrong answer here; as long as it's honest, a yes is just as good as a no.)

The second question is "Can you absolutely know that it's true?"

 Can I absolutely know that my brother is lost to me, yes or no? There's no maybe here, no prevaricating. Could I swear in a court of law that this statement is the truth, the whole truth, and nothing but the truth?

 No. (Actually, I cannot know that for sure.)

The third question is "How do you react, what happens, when you believe that thought?"

First, I feel furious. I want to punch something. And once the anger fades, I feel deep sadness. I miss the brother I knew.

The fourth question is "Who would you be without the thought?"
I'd feel more peaceful within myself. I'd be present to the Willie who is right in front of me. I'd notice that he's still alive, and I'd be free to appreciate that.

The last part of The Work is to turn the original statement around to the self, to the other, and to the opposite. Then give three specific examples of how the turnarounds are true in the same scenario.
Thus, the original statement, "My brother is lost to me," turns around to . . .
I am lost to me.

1. When I believe that Willie is lost, I get frantic and lose touch with my own peaceful center.
2. When I believe that Willie is lost, I behave in ways that are not consistent with my truest self—for example, I feel justified in ignoring him and not making contact.
3. When I believe that Willie is lost, what I'm really saying is that the brother I hold in my mind and heart isn't the same as the one in front of me. It's my projection, my construct of him that I've lost, not my actual, physical brother. So "I am lost to me" is actually more accurate because I created the version of my brother I think I've lost. It's part of me that I've lost, not him.

I am lost to my brother.

1. When I believe that Willie is lost, I don't reach out to him; I don't call or write or initiate conversation.
2. When I believe that Willie is lost, I have behaved in damaging ways; a few times when we were younger, I hit him back. I also ignored him at times. I've also moved far away from where he lives, so we rarely see one another. Frankly, it would be understandable if he felt he'd lost me.

3. When I believe that Willie is lost, I behave more like a distant parent and less like a sister; I communicate with our parents about his care, but I rarely communicate with him directly.

My brother is here with me.

1. On our family vacations, I can see that, physically, my brother is alive.
2. There are many moments when Willie is not upset, when he behaves in ways that are consistent with the brother I've known my whole life.
3. My brother lives in my mind and heart; we love each other, so we're always with each other.

5

You Don't Owe Anyone

Your Forgiveness

> The person who you are today must forgive your younger
> self for what she could not possibly have known yet at the
> time. It wasn't because she was stupid, or evil, or terrible . . .
> she had simply not taken that class yet. We are all just
> students in this classroom. We are all beginners.
> —Elizabeth Gilbert, Facebook, December 2014

HERE'S A WILD IDEA for you: What if you don't need to stop being a perfectionist? Right now, you may think that if you could just get rid of that perfectionist part of yourself, then you would be all right. But the truth is that you will only arrive at a felt sense of being "all right" when you accept yourself for who you really are. What if you could feel safe and loved even in the midst of the perfectionism? What if you could have the visceral knowledge that you can be uptight, obsessive, and controlling . . . and still beloved?

Fortunately, there's a way for us to get to that inner knowing; it's called self-forgiveness. Throughout the chapter, I'll share more about what this looks like, and I'll offer a specific practice at the end. But first, let's get honest about what it actually sounds like in your head here, now, today. What does it sound like when you're beating yourself up about something you've done or failed to do?

Maybe you're thinking,

/ *I can't believe I spent so long researching that movie online! I'm such a loser.*

/ *I forgot to write down that thing! I'm so messed up.*

/ *I didn't send that birthday gift yet! I'm such a bad friend.*

Perfectionists like us are really hard on ourselves. Early on, we learned to demand personal flawlessness because in some way it kept us safe. But that same behavior now only succeeds in tearing us down.

Instead of getting stuck in the shame-and-blame game, let's see how it feels to accept ourselves and offer ourselves forgiveness—for all of it.

Here's an example of how this looked for me recently, when I left a pot of rice cooking on the stove for too long. (Though I'm meticulous in most areas, I've had my fair share of cooking mishaps. Back in elementary school, I absentmindedly put a plastic plate in a toaster oven because I was eager to get back to a book and also because I was concerned about crumbs dropping from the bread to the burner below. Needless to say, the melted plastic plate made a much bigger mess than the crumbs would have.)

So when I realized what I'd done with the rice, my first reaction was frustration: *I can't believe I forgot again!* I didn't want to lift the lid and see that I'd ruined perfectly good food. I didn't want to have made a mistake.

And then it happened. Seven words slipped out of my mouth almost before I knew what I was saying: "I forgive myself for burning the rice."

That was it. But that was everything. In that moment, I realized that my default setting had changed from shame to self-forgiveness.

True, I said those words of self-forgiveness with some resignation, but I said them. And even more radically, I meant them. For a recovering perfectionist, that was a huge win. (As an added bonus, the rice wasn't burned after all. There was a tiny bit of water left, just enough to save the whole thing.)

So here's my question to you: How do you treat yourself when you make a mistake? Do you speak words of self-forgiveness, or are you harsh with yourself and others?

When you learn to forgive yourself, a whole new world opens up.

I'm already hearing the shame-based objection here: *Who am I to offer myself forgiveness? Doesn't that need to come from a Higher Power, from God?*

This might sound radical, but if you believe that God is Unconditional Love (which is biblical, by the way), then by definition there is no judgment coming at you from that Love. The definition of unconditional is "absolute; unqualified." Ergo, there is no room in Unconditional Love for judgment! It's 100 percent pure Love and 0 percent judgment.

You do not need to ask God for forgiveness because God isn't actually judging you. God is just doing God's job, which is to love you completely, radically, and unconditionally.

You, however, have been judging your own sweet self. As such, it makes sense to offer yourself forgiveness. You have the power to judge, and you also have the power to forgive. The choice is yours, moment by moment. Whatever it is that you're beating yourself up for, you don't need to do that. You don't need to hurt yourself anymore. You have suffered long enough. You don't need to keep stumbling under the weight of your own judgments. You don't need to do any more penance for the past.

I wish I would have known that when I was a teenager. I wish I'd understood that God wasn't ever judging me for the things I did when I was afraid.

I LOVE MY brother *so much I could run through the wall.* I wrote that line in first grade, and during our teenage years, it felt as though that was what was being asked of me. On a near-daily basis, I watched Willie hurt himself and our family. I watched him punch holes in walls, and I couldn't stop it from happening. I was scared to fall asleep in the room next door to Willie's, scared to wake up to the sound of him screaming in the middle of the night. I bore witness to his pain; I tried and failed to ease it. And then one day, I wasn't willing to watch anymore.

In the wake of yet another rage attack, Mom, Dad, our dog Curley, and I sprawled on the floor in the upstairs hallway. (Curley had hidden herself under Mom and Dad's bed when Willie had melted down, and she'd only just worked up the courage to come out.) We were all avoiding Willie, who was still downstairs rolled up in the living-room rug. I considered going to hide in my closet, but instead I took a breath and started talking.

"Mom, Dad, I need to talk to you," I said. "This can't keep happening. I can't do it. I can't watch Willie hurt himself and you anymore. He needs help. He needs to live somewhere else. *Please.*" My voice trembled and broke on the last word.

"Cari, it's OK," Dad said, but it wasn't OK.

"And where would he go?" Mom said, her voice sharp. "You think we haven't thought about it? If we took him to a hospital, do you know what they'd do? They'd just drug him until he was a vegetable. I can't do that to him."

"But he needs help, Mom," I said. "I don't know how. I don't know the system—but he needs professional help."

Mom was already shaking her head *No.*

I turned to my father, my last hope. "Dad, don't you think so?"

Dad's reply was reluctant but clear. "Yes, I do." He turned to Mom. "I've been thinking the same thing. Maybe Willie should live somewhere else."

He hears me! He agrees! Oh my God, maybe this could actually happen.

"I can't do that," Mom said. "I can't just give up on him. He's my *son.*"

"Then, maybe . . . may *I* please go live somewhere else? Just until I graduate? I know one of my friends would let me. Please?" I knew that the question would hurt my parents, but I had to try. Staying in that house felt scarier to me than leaving it.

"No, Caroline," Mom replied, with finality. "We are a *family*. We stay together."

—

A FEW MONTHS EARLIER, I'd begged Mom to take me to a dermatologist to consult about removing a few of my moles. I'd wanted them gone for ages, particularly one on my chest. Mom had agreed to schedule the appointment and accompany me there, but she wouldn't agree to a cosmetic removal.

At the appointment, the doctor had said, "Well, some of these moles are definitely bigger than we'd like them to be, particularly the one on your chest, but none look problematic. No need to take them out now, unless they're bothering you."

"But they *are* bothering me," I'd said, crossing my arms. The embarrassment of stripping down in front of a stranger and the mounting frustration of not getting what I wanted had made me bold.

"Well . . ." the doctor had hesitated, glancing over at Mom, "How about waiting until you're eighteen? Then it'll be your call." I'd scrambled back into my clothes in silence, willing myself not to cry. Why was the answer always no?

But after I'd initiated the conversation with my parents about either getting Willie into treatment or letting me move out, an idea occurred to me: *I can just cut the moles off myself. I can stop asking permission and start cutting.*

Immediately, I set some parameters: I would only cut moles in spots that were covered up by my clothes. No big deal. It wasn't a problem. I had friends who sliced at their wrists and arms with razors, but this was nothing like that, surely. My cuts wouldn't show. And I wouldn't use a razor.

So one day, I stepped out of the shower and searched below our mustard-yellow, seventies-style bathroom sink for rubbing alcohol and nail clippers. I targeted a mole on my upper arm. Quickly, before I could lose my nerve, I swabbed with alcohol and snipped away the mark. It stung, but the pain was nothing compared to the rush of exhilaration: *I did it! It's gone!* I felt so calm, so in control. I put on a Band-Aid and got dressed, feeling as though I'd really turned a corner.

A few days later, Willie's behavior went from bad to worse, and I found myself standing in the bathroom again. The next mole I wanted gone had the circumference of a pencil eraser. It was much bigger than the other mark I'd cut but still small enough to seem manageable. *Plus*, I reasoned, *my bra will conceal the bandage perfectly. No one will see it.*

Cutting was seductive; it was a way for me to rebel and hurt no one but myself. While Willie was hurting other people, I chose to contain the damage to my own body. It was just like Julie Barton wrote of her own family in *Dog Medicine*: "[My brother and I] were both hurting . . . and his way of coping with his pain was to turn to anger, to turn it toward me. My way of coping was to turn to sorrow and turn against myself." Cutting was me turning against myself.

Soon the day came when Willie lashed out in a particularly frightening fashion, leaving Mom and me both bruised as we tried to restrain him. Afterward I ran upstairs and closed the door of the bathroom. My body felt separate from my mind; it seemed as though I was watching my actions from up above.

There were my hands, shaking slightly as they turned the brass doorknob to lock it. There were my hands, steadier, more determined, opening and closing the familiar drawers. There were my hands, preparing the skin on the right side of my neck, where a large beauty mark rested just below my pulse point.

Beyond a vague thought to wear turtlenecks, I didn't consider concealment. I just cut. The pain was significant, but I breathed through it, keeping my slices controlled, careful. Soon the mole was gone, and my skin was red with blood again. *What have I done?*

"Caroline, you've been in there for a while. Are you OK?" My mom asked from outside the bathroom door.

When I didn't respond, she tried the knob. "Sweetie, are you OK?"

"I'm fine, Mom," I said, but I wasn't a good actress; my voice didn't sound right at all.

"Caroline, open the door *now.*" I unlocked the door with one hand while pressing the toilet paper to my bleeding neck with the other.

My mother stepped into the room, and our eyes met in the mirror. As I stared at our reflections, I was terrified by the realization that I actually wanted Mom to see what I'd done. Maybe I wasn't so different from my friends who sliced their arms with razors. Maybe I, too, was crying for help.

"Oh, *Caroline,*" she said. That was all.

Shame flushed my cheeks and filled my eyes. When I didn't speak— what could I possibly say that the blood on my neck didn't?—my mother turned away, closing the bathroom door behind her.

—

I DON'T KNOW WHY my mother walked away from me that day. But I do know that forgiving yourself begins with turning toward the part of you that is hurting the most right now.

If you're feeling overwhelmed at the prospect, that's understandable. Often this happens because you've deeply identified with the pain and self-judgment, so there's a need to create some space in your psyche. One practice I use involves connecting with these different aspects of consciousness, teasing out which part is judging and which part is hurting from the judgment. In that spirit, I want to offer you a really helpful model of human consciousness that I learned from Dr. Martha Beck.

First, imagine the part of you that is your Essential Self (or Wild Child). This is the human self that you were born with, the impulsive, heart-centered part of you that feels deeply. Next, picture the Social Self (or Dictator). This part of you is more rational, intellectual, planning-oriented, and sometimes judgmental. In your mind's eye, picture these two parts of you as actual entities, perhaps one perching on each shoulder. Allow them to take whatever form they take in your imagination. Neither one is wrong or bad; they just are.

When you're struggling to forgive yourself, it usually means that the Social Self and the Essential Self are at odds with each other. The Social Self is judging the Essential Self harshly, and the Essential Self is totally freaked out by the judgment. She's scared, so she acts out, which makes the Social Self judge her even more. The dynamic is akin to a parent yelling at a child who doesn't understand words yet. The parent gets angrier and angrier as the child gets more and more terrified.

This is what it felt like for me in high school, when my home felt so scary and I started cutting. My inner Wild Child was frantic to find some form of relief and rebellion that didn't hurt anyone else, and my inner Dictator was furious at her for being "weak," which then made her want to cut even more. It was a bad cycle.

Now that you're looking at your own Wild Child and Dictator, the question that you get to ask yourself is "Who am I in this scenario?"

Since you're able to observe them both, you can't really *be* one or the other. The more truthful answer is that you are the Watcher. You are the observing consciousness, the one who witnesses both aspects. Martha Beck refers to this observing consciousness as the Stargazer; it's the ever-present, peaceful part of you that is connected to all that ever was, is, and will be. It's the capital-*S* Self.

From the perspective of the Watcher, you can offer both the Wild Child and the Dictator some kindness. Speak whatever words feel like peace, like freedom. If it feels like too much of a stretch to say "I love you," you might start with something like "I see and acknowledge you both. I'm here to help you. I want the best for you."

You can also use this great affirmation from Christel Nani: "I fully love and accept all of me, even though I don't believe I am lovable." This seeming contradiction is freeing because it allows you to be honest about the tension of your old beliefs while still applying love to the parts of you that are hurting. I also love the way the sentence changes the more you say it. For me, it has become "I fully love and accept all of me; even though I don't believe, I am lovable."

In one sense, it does matter what you believe. Your beliefs directly influence how you feel and act, so of course they are important. However, in a more fundamental sense, it doesn't matter whether you do or do not believe that you are lovable at any given moment. The deeper truth is that you *are* lovable—period, end of story. Love is your true nature. It is immutable. It can be hidden or covered up but not changed.

Your only real challenge is to remember who you are.

IN THE FALL, my parents drove me north to Vassar, my first-choice college and culturally approved escape route. They arranged a rare day of respite care for Willie so that they could help me with move-in day. Yet however much I'd wished for our parents' undivided attention over the past two years, the actual experience made me feel strange and off-kilter. There was a disconnect between us; they thought that my first day at Vassar marked my first day on my own, but that didn't feel true for me. Emotionally, I'd been on my own ever since the day I realized that no matter how Willie behaved, they wouldn't seek another place for him—or me—to live.

When we said goodbye, Mom hugged me tight and left me a card replete with Bible verses. Dad made cheesy jokes and gave me multiple bear hugs. They were doing the best they could.

Freshman year wasn't easy—three girls in a single room never is—but despite our differences, my roommates I muddled through it together. I loved my classes, especially in English literature. And since there was no WCG congregation anywhere near Vassar, I dipped my toe in the water of Vassar's Intervarsity Christian Fellowship instead.

Fellowship was the first time that I'd worshipped with people from so many different denominations. The students who came to Tuesday-night meetings were Catholic, Protestant, Mormon, and everything in between. When we sang together, my childhood definition of heaven as a place without barriers came back to me.

Plus, I'd arrived at Vassar with a mission: to be better and more unselfish than I'd been back home. I'd be kind to everyone and be a witness for Christ. I wouldn't party, and I wouldn't drink. Instead, I would be on fire for Jesus. It was just that simple.

Except that it didn't turn out to be simple at all. Living in our dorm and trying to be "holy" meant every weekend felt just like my grade-school Halloweens, when I handed out candy while the other kids trick-or-treated. My Vassar peers were all drinking, and I stood on the metaphorical sideline with my Bible and Christian rock CDs. By Halloween of my freshman year, I'd had enough. With my roommates' encouragement, I dressed up as my alter ego "Bad Caroline," in a red lace dress and high-heeled boots. And when they offered me Smirnoff Ice, I said yes. I sang along to songs with curse words in them and danced dirty with a guy I liked.

But once Bad Caroline went back into the box, our brief romance ended; by spring, I heard that he was dating someone else. I coped with this news by putting on more makeup, formfitting jeans, and a tight, white mesh tank top that I thought made me look tough. As the final step in my transformation, I drank all of the beer that I was offered.

That was how it was for me in college: I was Good Caroline, fulfilling all of my responsibilities to everyone right up until I got too sad or too tired or both. Then I slipped into being Bad Caroline, the one who drank and danced like the people in the music videos Mom hadn't allowed me to watch. There was a split between those two sides of me, between singing on the worship team and dancing at clubs, leading Bible studies and taking shots of tequila.

My roommates had no such inner conflict; they were thrilled at the return of Bad Caroline. Together, we trotted tipsily to a party in my friend Brooke's dorm. When we heard the distinctive opening chant and siren noises of "Shake Ya Tailfeather," the three of us threw our arms over our heads. Dancing my way through a crowded doorway, I spotted Brooke across the room. "Brookie! Hello Brookie, my Brooke!"

Brooke and I were both English majors, oldest daughters, and diligent achievers prone to stress-related illness. I trusted her with my papers and my perfectionism, my hopes and my fears.

Brooke's face lit up when she saw us. "Yay, you guys made it!"

I leaned over for a hug. "I love this song! It's my jam!"

Tilting her head a little to one side and assessing me with a concerned gaze, she said, "How many drinks have you had, honey?"

I held my thumb and forefinger apart just a little bit, smiling broadly.

"Right, OK," Brooke said, turning to my roommates. "How many has she had, really?"

Their reply was lost in the din.

"Hey, how about you drink water now? Here, I'll get you some," Brooke said, ducking down and pouring water from a battered Brita pitcher into a plastic cup.

"No, no," I said, bypassing the cup and pouring myself a shot of cheap vodka. "This is yummy!"

What I didn't say was that water was too good for me. Water was for people who saved all of their kisses for marriage and were sold-out for Jesus. I deserved to swallow something that hurt my throat and made my eyes water.

The next day, when I was so catastrophically hungover that I had to break individual Cheerios in half in order to keep them down, I remembered how Brooke had held out the water for me. She'd done so with kindness and without judgment. I thought about how my friend had deemed me worthwhile when I hadn't been able to believe it myself.

I felt safe with Brooke, who reassured me when I went into paroxysms of shame after the occasional night of drinking. For me, partying was a terrible double bind: If I didn't do it, I felt the same kind of loneliness and separation from my peers I'd felt growing up. If I did do it, then I felt as though I'd failed God.

But Brooke would say, "Cari, I really don't think that God is mad at you. I'm not, anyway. I love you. You're my *person*," she'd emphasize, quoting our favorite line from *Grey's Anatomy*. "And you'll feel better when you get some of the alcohol out of your system. Here, drink more water."

BETWEEN GOOD CAROLINE AND Bad Caroline, there were visits home to my parents and Willie. I brought laundry home, but I also tried to help out; I'd offer to take care of Willie so our parents could have a break.

But one day when our parents were out, he started melting down and things got out of hand. I prompted him to roll up in the oriental rug and tried to apply calming pressure, but it didn't help. Willie had left enough room between himself and the rug to resist, and he thrashed so much that I lost my footing.

"What the hell?" I gasped, trying desperately to keep him rolled up. "Willie, Willie, you need to stay here, OK? You need to get calm."

At that, he launched his body upward, throwing off the rug entirely. Too late, I saw him lunging toward me. I managed a few frantic steps into the front hall, but I wasn't fast enough. Willie grabbed me and sank his teeth hard into my calf.

Falling to the hallway floor and landing on my knees, I screamed, "Get off me, get off me! Shit! Shit!"

I kicked and thrashed as hard as I could, but Willie just held on and bit down harder. Finally, adrenaline propelled me to yank my leg away and rush up the stairs and into our parents' bedroom— *There's a phone there, I'll call for help.* I barely locked the door in time; Willie pounded his fists against the wood as I sobbed and gasped. I could feel my throat constricting as hyperventilation took over. *You have plenty of air, just breathe*, I coached myself.

Still, my breath sped and stuttered. I balled my hands into fists and made myself a fierce promise, one that helped me slow my breath at last: *I will go back to Vassar as soon as Mom and Dad get here. I will drive back and go to my room and lock the door, and I won't come back here for a long, long time.*

When I'd calmed down enough to breathe normally, I picked up the phone and dialed Mom's cell. "Mom, Willie had a bad meltdown," I said without preamble. "I tried to help him get into the rug but it didn't work. And then he bit me." My voice wobbled, but I fought for control, sounding robotic as I said, "You need to come home. I need to leave now."

"Oh no! Oh, Caroline," Mom said. Then, as an aghast aside to Dad, "*He bit her.*" Then, "We'll be right there. Are you safe now?"

"Yes. I locked myself in your room."

"Good girl. What's Willie doing?"

"I think he's breaking drinking glasses on the back deck."

"You know he's done that before. Just stay where you are. We're coming right home."

For the next hour, I sat still on the edge of our parents' bed. As soon as I heard the garage door open, I jolted into motion. I grabbed my bags and rushed down the stairs, out the front door, and into the driveway. I walked right to my forest-green Dodge Stratus, which I'd nicknamed "Dodgy" in a lighthearted mood I couldn't imagine regaining.

"Cari, honey, wait," Mom called across the driveway.

"I'm sorry. I can't. I have to go. I'm sorry," I said, tossing my bag into the backseat of the car and racing to the front seat.

"Oh, sweetie," she said, sadness in every line of her face. "I'm sorry you're upset. We love you."

I didn't reply. By the time I pulled my car onto campus, I didn't feel much of anything aside from the persistent throbbing in my calf.

Still I didn't think to go to Health Services at Vassar. What would I have said to a nurse, anyway? *My brother goes insane sometimes and hurts people, and today he bit me really hard. But I convinced our parents to let me watch him by myself, so it's my fault for being an idiot?*

No. Instead I limped to my dorm, grabbed an ice pack from the minifridge, and stared at the ceiling of my room.

Days later, I opened my campus mailbox to find a letter from my family. Mom and Dad had written words of love and sorrow, and a single sheet of white, lined paper bore my brother's distinctive printing: "Dear Caroline, I'm very sorry I bit you. Please forgive me. Love, Willie."

I didn't cry. Instead I traced the places where Willie had pressed the pen into the paper, as though force could atone for force.

I wondered if I could forgive him, then realized that wasn't the issue. The real question was whether I could forgive myself.

IF YOU'RE OPEN TO self-forgiveness but you aren't sure where to start, one place to begin is the deeply uncomfortable feeling I call "weird shame."

Weird shame is the feeling that you've done something wrong—that you *are* wrong—but you have no idea where it originates. You feel bad, but you're not sure why.

The key here is to get curious about the weird shame rather than stuff it down. As we talked about earlier, even so-called negative feelings have natural buoyancy; no matter how much we push them down, they're going to come up eventually. So we might as well work with them.

If you're game to explore, just sit with the weird shame for a little while. Set a timer for five minutes, and give it some space. Find out what, exactly, you're judging and shaming yourself for in the first place.

Spoiler alert: you probably will not like sitting with the shame. (And if you're feeling anxious that it might be too much to take on alone, please reach out to a trusted support person.) Just remember that you do not have to do anything except keep breathing, and look inward when you can. You can take a break whenever you need to; you do not need to rush or force anything. This practice is about creating space for your own truth to rise to the surface.

When you're ready, ask the questions, "Weird shame, where are you coming from? What are you trying to tell me?"

I did this practice recently, when some weird shame arose after some old friends attended a coaching webinar I'd hosted online.

The source of the weird shame wasn't immediately obvious because my instinctive reaction to recognizing those friends on the attendee list was joyful.

Yet as soon as I let myself ask that question, "Weird shame, where are you coming from?" the issue became clear.

The friends who showed up to my webinar were people who knew me back in college. They knew me when I tried hard to be Super Christian Caroline, when I believed things that I no longer believe. When I drank too much and hurt myself on purpose. When I had anxiety attacks and shame spirals. When I was, in some ways, lost.

All at once, it made sense: The weird shame wasn't about my friends at all. It was about my own judgment of Past Caroline.

Instantly, I identified the painful thought: "If people really knew me, they'd turn away." But the truth was that those friends did know me, and they didn't turn away. On the contrary, they showed up more than a decade later to attend my webinar!

They didn't judge me. Only I judged me. Fortunately, I didn't have to stay in judgment, and neither do you.

THE NO-OWE INVITATION

Offer Yourself Forgiveness—and Mean It

This is a continuation of the exercises from the previous two chapters. Once you've identified your projections, judgments, and limiting beliefs, you have an opportunity to offer yourself forgiveness. Here is the process I learned from the counseling team at The Clearing, originally taught by Drs. Ron and Mary Hulnick in their spiritual psychology program at the University of Santa Monica.

To do self-forgiveness work, first connect with your loving heart. Focus on a deep, true connection; feel it in your heart's center. One way to do this is to take yourself to an internal place where you feel deeply safe and peaceful. You might imagine a physical space in nature or perhaps holding a pet or a loved one close. Whatever you choose, aim for a felt experience of unconditional love. (If that feels really challenging, it's OK; just do the best you can. Don't let perfectionism stop you from doing the rest of the exercise.)

Once you're grounded in that loving, positive energy, set an intention to heal. You may have different words you want to use, but do speak your words out loud. For example, you might say, "My intention is to heal at the deepest level possible."

Next, write down your self-judgments and limiting beliefs. Don't hold back by pretending to be nicer to yourself than you really are.

If you judge yourself as selfish, lazy, bad, or horrible, then write that down. If you think you'll always be bad and you'll never change, write that down too.

Once you've done that, make sure that you're holding the energy of love as you speak your new truths out loud.

For judgments, use this script: "I forgive myself for judging myself as [fill in the blank], and the truth is [fill in the blank]."

Fill in the first blank with your judgment and the second blank with the truth from the standpoint of unconditional love. Pick words that resonate with your sense of integrity. You do not need to state the opposite of the judgment if that doesn't feel true for you yet. Instead, go with a statement that actually resonates with you.

Here are some examples from my own life:

- I forgive myself for judging myself as a failure, and the truth is that I'm human, and I'm doing the best that I can.
- I forgive myself for judging myself as broken, and the truth is that I am loved and I am strong.
- I forgive myself for judging myself as a terrible person, and the truth is that I'm just me. And just being me is OK.

For limiting beliefs, use this script: "I forgive myself for accepting the limiting belief that [fill in the blank], and the truth going forward for me is [fill in the blank]." Again, fill in the first blank with your limiting belief and the second blank with the truth from the standpoint of unconditional love. For example,

- I forgive myself for accepting the limiting belief that I'll never be good enough, and the truth going forward for me is that there is no one holding a scorecard but me, and I can drop it anytime I want to. The truth going forward for me is that I choose to drop the scorecard. I am free, and I choose to enjoy my freedom.

Whenever your old beliefs arise, speak your newfound truths out loud. As you practice the new beliefs, you may find it helpful to keep the rewrites close at hand in a notebook. At first it will feel strange, but stick with it. You've had years of practice with being mean to yourself, so kindness is a big change. Trust the process. This exercise gives you an accessible way to practice self-compassion, which then overflows into every relationship in your life.

6

You Don't Owe Anyone

Superhuman Strength

The life of a caretaker is as addictive as the life of an
alcoholic. Here the intoxication is the emotional relief
that temporarily comes when answering a loved one's
need. Though it never lasts, in the moment of answering
someone's need, we feel loved. While much good can come
from this, especially for those the caretaker attends, the
care itself becomes a drink by which we briefly numb a
worthlessness that won't go away unless constantly doused
by another shot of self-sacrifice.

—Mark Nepo, *The Book of Awakening*

HAVE YOU EVER PLAYED that game where you do your best to
remember something—a song, a poem, an address—that you knew by
heart a long time ago? If so, then you know that this game is most
compelling when you're avoiding what you're "supposed to" be doing.
You tell yourself that of course you'll tackle that challenging project, just as soon as you've sung all of the Backstreet Boys songs from
their first album and recited your middle-school friends' home phone
numbers.

It's not just you, I promise; the other day during meditation, my mind decided that instead of being still, I needed to see if I could still recite the Ten Commandments in order. I started off strong: "Thou shalt not have any other gods before me." I made it to the last one—don't covet—when I realized that I'd only named nine. I must have forgotten one somewhere in the middle—what was it? I pondered for a moment before the answer popped up. I'd missed number three, "Remember the Sabbath day by keeping it holy."

This did not register as a random mistake.

If you're a self-help junkie like me and you've spent any length of time reading up on productivity, then you know that the standard guidance is geared toward getting more done. And some days, that is really helpful. There are times when we need motivational, get-up-and-go, eat-that-frog pep talks.

Yet there are times when we need something different. There are times when our productivity is actually the problem, not the solution. Modern American culture is imbued with the belief that hard work can fix anything. But what if you're already a hard worker and you have trouble resting? What if your struggle is not in flipping the switch on but in turning it off?

In my experience, it's hard for us recovering perfectionists to—how shall I say this most eloquently?—take a freaking break already. Even if we've planned to pause, even if we've marked an hour or a day off on our calendar, we feel very uneasy about stopping our work. Coloring outside the lines of a productive routine is difficult for us. We like to think of ourselves as superhuman, and resting "extra" messes with that self-concept. (In our book, working extra is virtuous and resting extra is dubious.)

During a therapy session in my late twenties, I told my counselor how scary it was for me to take a break from my daily disciplines. I shared with her how even if I skipped a day of exercise or writing for a really good reason, it still freaked me out.

"You know," she responded, "it's a leap of faith to nurture yourself if your default setting is to work harder."

That one sentence gave me permission to think differently. From then on, I began reframing days away from work as leaps of faith, not laziness.

You are allowed to do this too. You get to remember that you are not a machine but rather a human animal. And you get to take care of yourself as you'd take care of another human being. Think about it: You'd never deny a small child adequate rest, nourishment, and playtime, right? So why would you deny yourself those basic things? There is a small child living within you, and that child is in your care.

How can this be? As adults, we are all a bit like Russian nesting dolls in that we carry our younger selves within us. As Madeleine L'Engle wrote in *A Circle of Quiet,*

> I am still every age that I have been. Because I was once a child, I am always a child. Because I was once a searching adolescent, given to moods and ecstasies, these are still part of me, and always will be. . . . This does not mean that I ought to be trapped or enclosed in any of these ages . . . but that they are in me to be drawn on; to forget is a form of suicide; my past is part of what makes the present Madeleine and must not be denied or rejected or forgotten.

When we forget our younger selves, it wounds us deeply, even kills; as L'Engle notes, this forgetting is a kind of psychological suicide. Whereas when we remember that we are still the child, we are more likely to take care of ourselves as adults.

With that said, it's not easy to do this. Our culture, our churches, and our families all condition us to sacrifice ourselves. Plus, when we first connect with those younger parts of ourselves, there's a backlog of pain waiting. We encounter needs that weren't met, hurts that weren't healed. It can be very tempting to avoid that backlog and abdicate responsibility for our emotional well-being to someone else instead.

Many—dare I say, most—problems in our relationships boil down to this: We want other people to take better care of ourselves than we do. We want *them* to read our minds, anticipate our needs, and shower us with unconditional love. If only *they* could do this, we reason, then all would be well. We want them to take care of us so that we don't have to do it!

You might think that for you it's the reverse, that if only you could take better care of *them*, if only *they* were happy, then *you* would be

OK. But whether you demand that other people meet your needs or martyr yourself to meet theirs, the core problem is the same: you're still abandoning yourself.

So then the question becomes, How do we stop abandoning ourselves? How do we learn to take care of ourselves first?

Let's begin with the realization that you don't owe anyone superhuman strength. You don't owe anyone taking on more than you can do with integrity. Going beyond your integrity forces you to deny who you are and how you're made. You don't have to lie about how much you can do. You are allowed to be human, period.

In my experience, people in caregiving roles are particularly vulnerable to the superhuman mythology. Taking care of other people's bodies is vital, holy work—and it's dangerous work too. It's neverending, and it can drown you if you let it. Taking care of others can be a profound spiritual practice, certainly. Yet it can also be a convenient spiritual bypass, a socially sanctioned way to avoid taking care of yourself.

I didn't have that perspective when I started my first job after college. Instead of going to New York and working in publishing like I'd planned, I impulsively signed up for an Americorps year of service at L'Arche Washington DC, a community that cared for adults with disabilities. My new job meant living alongside individuals with intellectual and developmental disabilities, providing hands-on care as part of an intentional community. The role resonated with me as a way to make meaning out of my brother's suffering. If I couldn't help Willie, at least I could help other men and women with special needs. At least I could use what I'd learned as Willie's sister to serve others.

On my first day at L'Arche, I met a man named Raymond, one of six "core members," the L'Arche term for the adults with disabilities at the center of community life. Raymond was the only one who used a wheelchair. Initially I found his face formidable, with its broad nose and blunt features. But then I noticed how it softened when the direct-care assistants lowered the lights and lit candles for prayer. And when he reached out his wide-palmed hand to me and murmured, "Shake-a-hand?" his touch was gentle. Throughout the prayer time, he made a loud purring noise that I couldn't have replicated if I'd tried. "That means he's happy," another assistant told me.

Compared to Willie's rages, none of the core members' medical issues or personal quirks intimidated me. *Maybe being Willie's sister prepared me for this role*, I thought. *Garbled speech and random purring? Bring it on. As long as no one's getting black eyes, I'm happy.*

Even so, my eyes widened when I saw the level of detail in the core members' morning routines; Raymond's alone ran one and a half pages, single-spaced. His care was detailed right down to the exact recipe for his oatmeal.

"I know it seems like a lot," said Jake, the experienced assistant assigned to train me on Raymond's routine. "But once you learn more about Raymond, you'll see how important the details are. He has a high level of medical need, so we need to be careful."

As we entered Raymond's warm, sunlit bedroom, Jake greeted him good morning. Raymond repeated the greeting, then let loose with that unusual purr. It was a resonant, glad buzzing that filled up the space. Then Jake helped Raymond strip off his nightclothes.

I averted my eyes reflexively, then forced myself to watch. All the while, Jake was in motion, donning latex gloves and arranging a bright yellow and orange beach towel on the seat of Raymond's wheelchair. He kept up a running commentary for my benefit: "Once he's in the wheelchair, always buckle the seat belt, click the wedge into place, and put his feet on the seat rests. Don't slack on that. It isn't safe otherwise."

I nodded, taking notes while my mind whirred with new information.

We made our way to the bathroom, where Jake ran the water until it got warm, transferred Raymond to the plastic shower chair, then helped Raymond lather up. Humid air filled the room, the vent fan circulating scents of bleach and soap and male bodies. Raymond purred again, and the white suds of his shampoo made a sort of halo in his hair. He was totally unashamed that a stranger was watching him shower. In fact, Raymond was literally vibrating with happiness. When Jake washed the shampoo away, Raymond chuckled and beamed.

Standing there in the soap-scented steam, I had the strangest feeling, a flush of something close to envy. Had I ever felt so at home in my own body, so profoundly content just being myself? Raymond was physically weak and dependent, but he had joy in himself. He didn't seem to mind receiving help or judge himself for needing it.

THEY SAY THAT WHEN the student is ready, the teacher appears. And so it was that I had two teachers that first year at L'Arche. Raymond taught me that it was possible to find joy in vulnerability, and Harley taught me where I myself was vulnerable and weak.

I thought that coming to L'Arche was a chance to leave my old pain behind. But even though I'd stopped cutting, I was still very good at hurting myself. I thought that punishing myself was part of love, even a prerequisite. In short, I had a lot to learn.

Harley was a new L'Arche assistant like me. The first time I met him, I walked away smiling—he was cute—but I also had an old kid's song called "You're in Trouble" playing in my mind. When Harley asked me out a few weeks later, I said yes impetuously. I ignored the old song's message and my common sense, both of which warned me I might regret dating a fellow assistant who'd told me his traumas when we were still strangers. What can I say? It was not a wise decision. But it was summer in DC, we liked the same books, and I was high on the feeling of a fresh start.

Our relationship had the feeling of a fairy tale. I was swept off my feet, head over heels, blinded by the light. It seemed that Harley was even more besotted; he slipped love notes under my door in the mornings and asked permission to meet my family. He was by my side constantly, eager and adoring. Even in the early haze of infatuation, though, I felt an uncomfortable twist in my stomach when I realized, *He likes me, yes, but he* really *doesn't like to be alone.*

Have you ever had an experience like that—one in which your mind didn't fully register a red flag, but your body did? If so, then you know that it's difficult to listen to your body when you've been trained to discount its signals. When you've spent years overriding feelings of discontent or aversion in order to please other people, you're out of touch with your natural instincts. This makes you tremendously vulnerable to exploitation. If you have trouble sensing the "something's off here" signal, you're in trouble. Instead of trusting your body's wisdom when it says *Danger, don't go there!,* you immediately rationalize what's making you uncomfortable and then blame yourself.

That's what I did when Harley wanted constant togetherness. I told myself the same things that my mom had told me, with the same shaming tone: *You're spending too much time alone with your books! Don't you want to be with people? You need to get out of your shell!* When something felt off in the dynamic, I assumed that I was the problem.

Yet Heather Havrilesky said it well: "Men who are secure with themselves can tolerate getting to know people slowly. They don't mind being alone. They make decisions and don't go back on them over and over again."

Within weeks, Harley ended our whirlwind relationship, ostensibly to get back together with his ex-girlfriend. I did not take it well. I yelled at him, paraphrasing *The Princess Bride* and calling him a coward with a heart full of fear. Then I locked myself in my room and collapsed. I was furious with him but even more so with myself; I told myself over and over that I should have known better.

I coped with the sudden breakup in the same way that I had with Willie's meltdowns: by throwing myself into achievement and occasionally hyperventilating in my closet. After a day or so of searing anger and silent treatment toward Harley, I did what I knew how to do and pushed the "bad" feelings down. I tried very hard to be calm, mature, and most of all, spiritual.

Admittedly, I did this partly for image control. The L'Arche community was still new to me, and I didn't want to be the sad, weak girl who couldn't get over a breakup. I thought I owed them superhuman strength. And I also thought that if I was just *better* in some undefinable way, then perhaps Harley would love me again.

If you've ever been through a sudden, significant loss, then you know how desperately the mind tries to make sense of it. When there's no obvious explanation for a relationship breakdown, many of us people-pleasers and perfectionists assume that it must be our fault. Being "wrong" feels awful, but it's also familiar and therefore somewhat safe. When we're the problem, it gives us a false but seductive sense of control. Maybe if we can perfect ourselves, then the other person will see the light!

But the truth is that we are not all-powerful. We are not superhuman. We do not control the minds, hearts, and actions of those around us. Other people's choices aren't really "about" us at all.

In her book *Inner Bonding,* author and therapist Margaret Paul recounts a conversation with a client whose date stood her up:

"It seems that you are taking it personally, believing it is your fault that he didn't show up.... Do you think it's possible that you are not the only one he had ever done this to?"

"I haven't thought about that. All I know is that he did it to me and I feel like there is something wrong with me."

"So if there was nothing wrong with you, then no one would ever let you down? All you have to do is find the right way to be and you can have complete control over others not disappointing you?"

That was the faulty belief I subscribed to when I was at L'Arche. I thought that if I could just find the right way to be, then I wouldn't be disappointed again.

———

WHEN I FELT SAD and lost, I sought refuge by visiting Raymond's room. Sitting by his side was the one place that felt peaceful to me. Most days, I'd knock on his door frame and he'd nod a greeting, then go back to shuffling his beloved alphabet blocks or flipping through his stack of magazines. We didn't talk much, but he held a space for me. He didn't seem to judge me or anyone else, so visiting him gave me a break from the hard, constant work of "being strong." Sometimes we'd watch small birds dance through the branches outside, beholding a ballet that most people missed. Mainly I'd just bask in his presence like someone with seasonal affective disorder in front of a light box.

When I'd start his morning routine at 6:30 a.m., Raymond would be awake already. At first, I'd been afraid to give Raymond a morning shower—what if I made a terrible mistake and he fell?—but then I'd taken to singing Sarah McLachlan's version of the Prayer of St. Francis as I helped him soap up. It helped me feel focused and grounded, and it seemed to bring Raymond joy; when I sang, he would buzz and chuckle and smile up at me.

And in the evening, after helping everyone through their tooth-brushing and flossing and nightly physical therapy exercises, I'd climb the stairs to my bedroom, which was located directly above Raymond's. This meant that sometimes I responded to urgent calls of "Bathroom!" that no one else could hear, but it also meant that a lullaby of purrs sang me to sleep each night. It felt like cosmic recompense for those fear-filled nights spent sleeping next door to Willie.

Each day, my respect for Raymond grew. He had every reason to be bitter and withdrawn, but he wasn't. Though he was dealt a difficult hand from birth—he was no stranger to pain, illness, or the ICU—he was a teacher of peace.

His body was weak, but his spirit was strong. He risked vulnerability; he welcomed everyone. No matter who visited our home or smiled at us at Starbucks, he wanted to shake their hands. He greeted people without hesitation, without inhibition. Initially, though, I didn't understand the risks involved in this way of being. I didn't understand that holding out his hand was a gamble because I couldn't imagine anyone turning away. How could anyone resist Raymond's wholehearted enthusiasm?

But then one day at Starbucks, I saw it happen. Raymond extended his hand, beaming up at the businessman in his tailored suit. The man stared back, but his gaze was cold. I saw him taking in Raymond's wheelchair and his obvious differences. Without a word, the man purposefully turned his back and turned away. Raymond's hand stayed outstretched, but his face fell.

I very much wanted to punch that guy in the face. Instead I sat on my trembling hands and turned to Raymond, who calmly went back to sipping his coffee. He handled the rejection better than I did, shaking it off and moving on with his life. In doing so, he taught me what strength looks like: to risk reaching out, yes, and also to love oneself enough to let go when someone else doesn't reach back.

SADLY, I DID NOT heed Raymond's wise example. If anything marred the happiness of that first autumn and winter at L'Arche, it was my inability to give up on the dream of getting back together with

Harley. We still saw each other every day. He was back with his ex, but we were still good friends. This was torture for me, but it seemed to work well for him.

I coped by continually asking myself, *What's wrong with me and how can I fix it?* I threw myself into being the best caregiver I could be. I lost weight. For a while I acted like I didn't care, then I wrote Harley a letter saying that I very much did. Worse yet, I actually gave him the letter. I was good at reaching out but not at letting go.

If you've ever done something like this, then you know how exhausting and humiliating it is. Every day, I tried my best to be poised, articulate, and fun. It was a months-long audition, a constant internal hustle to regain a role I'd already lost. It was nothing like Raymond's lived example; it was the polar opposite of peace.

Now I know that there are times when no matter how much you care about the other person, it's not loving to yourself to try and resurrect that relationship. There are times when you need to recognize, *Wait a minute, this relationship I want so desperately is actually really unhealthy for me.* But there is a payoff to working hard. When you still have something to fix, then you get to avoid your grief. Striving to "improve" yourself means that you can sidestep the painful reality: it's over.

When that realization finally dawned on me at Christmastime, I hit the self-destruct button. This time, self-abuse didn't take the form of cutting or binge drinking, but overwork. Once more, hurting myself gave me a sense of control. Harley had hurt me, I thought, but maybe *I* could hurt me worse. I switched out one form of self-harm for another; caregiving became my new addiction. I didn't set boundaries with work. I never said no to a request. I gave all day long—twelve-, thirteen-, fourteen-hour days—then I collapsed into bed at night and stared at the ceiling, unable to sleep. Sleep involves surrender, and I was not yet ready for surrender.

By February, I developed a blistering, knifepoint painful rash on my upper left rib cage. When I finally dragged myself to a doctor, he flinched at the sight of my skin. Without meeting my eyes, he scribbled on a chart and made a diagnosis: "It's shingles, no question."

"What? I thought older people got shingles. I'm twenty-two."

"Older people do tend to get it more often, but hey, it's DC. Stress is a trigger. I see plenty of cases in young professionals, especially politicians."

When I heard that, the haze of denial dissipated, allowing me to see clearly. For months, I'd been trying so hard to get Harley to see me as someone worthy of his love. I'd purposefully exhausted myself on a grueling campaign trail, and it wasn't worth it. It had never been worth it.

After the shingles diagnosis, I changed course. I started meditating, going to bed earlier, and keeping my distance from Harley. All of those things helped me heal. But still, I ended up with a ropy, raised scar just below my heart. Whenever I let myself get stressed or overworked, the nerves on my upper left rib cage would burn out a warning: *Slow down or pay the price.*

MEANWHILE I FIELDED CALLS from my mom, with my dad in the background. Willie was still hurting them and himself. One day he melted down in public, hitting Mom and scaring a playground full of children in the process. When she told me about the incident during one of our conversations, I felt my entire being freeze in horror.

"Mom, are you OK?" I managed to ask. I scuffed my foot hard against the green wall-to-wall carpeting of my bedroom at L'Arche, thinking that these conversations never got easier however often we repeated them.

Her response? "Oh no, I'm OK. I'm fine. It was just traumatic, that's all."

Those contradictory words made no sense to me, but I couldn't think of a polite way to say so. I was tempted to put down the phone, to listen instead to the rustling of new green leaves outside my window and the faint purrs and chuckles coming from Raymond's room below. In my spacious third-floor room, I wanted to keep a sense of refuge and sanctuary. I wanted to avoid bringing the latest scary story into this peaceful place.

But I didn't do that. I thought I had to be strong enough to hear the same heartbreaking account again and again rather than drawing a line and saying, "No more." Instead of doing that, I made plans with my parents to go on a family vacation to South Carolina.

THE TROUBLE ON OUR trip didn't start with a dramatic meltdown from Willie, though. It began with a simple evening walk from our hotel to the beach, with Mom, Dad, Willie, and I walking along a sandy footpath to the shoreline. At times we could walk two abreast, but more often the path narrowed, and we went single file. Willie walked in front, as usual. Dad followed, presumably to keep an eye on Willie when we came to the highway crossing. I walked a slight distance behind Willie and Dad, and Mom followed me.

As we strolled, I looked up at the sky, which was beginning to take on the rosy hues of sunset. I listened to the calling of the seagulls and felt the sun warming my pale skin. I took deep breaths of the salty air, thinking, *God, it's so good to take a break.* For a few moments, all I felt was peace.

But then I glanced back at Mom a few yards behind me. She didn't say a word, but I felt her dismay as surely as though she'd shouted it across the distance. Instantly, I thought, *I should hang back to keep her company.*

It was an automatic thought, born from years of experience. When my introverted need for alone time conflicted with Mom's extroverted need for interaction, I'd try to spend as much time with her as possible. That day, though, I didn't follow the usual script. After nearly a year of living in a L'Arche home with twelve housemates, I did not want to surrender my solo time on the walk.

As Mom caught up to the rest of us on the beach, her shoulders were shaking with sobs.

"Honey, what is it? What's wrong?" Dad asked.

"Mom, are you OK? Are you hurt?" I asked.

Mom took a breath and faced me, saying forcefully, "Yes! I'm hurt because you didn't walk with me. You left me *alone*! I just wish that my only daughter would love me and want to walk with me." She sniffed and swiped at her cheeks.

My stomach dropped. Hadn't I felt the telltale stab of guilt for not anticipating her emotional needs? Had I done the wrong thing, ignoring that guilt? Or was there a problem with the expectation itself?

THAT INCIDENT MADE ME look more closely at my relationship with my mom and the dynamic we'd created over the years. Through stepping back and creating a new life for myself at L'Arche, I had a different perspective. Time and distance helped me see what I hadn't seen before.

I know it's hard to open your eyes in this way. When you begin noticing the troubled relationships in your life, often there's an impulse to turn away from what is true. There's a tendency to deny, to insist that your friendships, family, or romantic relationships are just fine—or at least, they *should* be, any minute now! Yet as Ayodeji Awosika wrote in his book *Real Help*, "The biggest obstacle to clarity is focusing on the way things *should work* as opposed to how they *do work*."

It takes courage to notice your troubled relationships and to let yourself name them for what they are. When you see that something isn't right, it is enormously helpful to have precise language to describe what's happening. (That said, naming particular dynamics is emphatically *not* the same as diagnosing the people involved in them. Psychologists and psychiatrists excepted, that's not our job.)

Here are some terms to illuminate what was going on beneath the surface in the story I've just shared, as well as several other definitions that have been extremely helpful for me and my clients. The list is by no means exhaustive; rather, it's a starting point to support you in identifying trouble spots in your own life. If these dynamics have played a significant role in your relationships, please learn more about them and seek support. (If you're not sure where to start, the works cited page at the end of the book lists several resources from which I've sourced the following terms.)

⟋ *Emotional caretaking or codependency* (also referred to as "relationship addiction") occurs when people abdicate responsibility for their own emotional needs and rely on others to meet them. In codependency, one person relies on another as an emotional caretaker, and together they create an unhealthy pattern. The emotional caretaker enables the more overtly irresponsible individual by shielding them from the consequences of their actions. Yet the irresponsible person may also enable the caretaker to avoid themselves and their own needs.

⟋ *Parentification* is an emotionally abusive role reversal in which young children become physical or emotional caregivers for their parents or siblings.

⟋ *Psychological abuse or emotional abuse* happens when one person attempts to control, shame, or hurt another via the use of emotions and psychological manipulations.

⟋ *The expectation of mind reading* occurs when someone in your life expects you to understand exactly what they want without them communicating their desire. It's a controlling behavior that discounts your separateness and your reality. When you invariably fail to anticipate their need or desire, the other person gets upset. Their behavior may tip the line into abuse. In a healthy adult-to-adult relationship, each adult is responsible for getting their own needs met and for directly communicating their desires.

⟋ *Psychologically and emotionally abusive behaviors* include, but are not limited to the following: gaslighting (when one person purposefully denies reality as a power play, with the intent to create confusion and doubt within the other person), denial and minimizing (acting as though the abuse is no big deal), and guilt-tripping (actively working to elicit guilt within the other person so as to manipulate them). Other behaviors that overlap with verbal abuse include unfair blame, belittling, name-calling, constant motive-questioning, and harsh criticism.

Many of us have minimized any abuse that isn't physical; however, we now know that verbal and emotional abuse can be just as damaging, if not more so. A 2014 study released by the American Psychological Association concluded that "children who are emotionally abused and neglected face similar and sometimes worse mental health problems as children who are physically or sexually abused." And as therapist Pete Walker writes in his book *The Tao of Fully Feeling*, "The combination of verbal and emotional abuse is the most lethal weapon used in the destruction of children's self-esteem."

Yes, you can heal. But first you must recognize the harm that was done.

JUST AS IT'S VITAL to name the dysfunctional behaviors, it's also important to name the patterns that bring peace. When we're able to identify the places of healing—to say, "This feels true and right for me"—we gain strength. We don't have to hustle for that peace; rather, we simply notice what nourishes and begin turning toward it.

That's one reason why living with Raymond was so profoundly healing for me: he was a master at holding space for others without pulling on them emotionally. I felt no pressure whatsoever to be a certain way with him. I could cry with him and laugh with him, talk or not talk, it didn't matter.

Some people might look at Raymond and think that he was trapped—in his wheelchair, in his body, in his dependency on others. But I knew that his spirit was strong and free. I knew that because living with him helped me feel that way too.

That's how you can tell real strength from counterfeit strength: You can feel it in your body. You can feel what it's like to push and pretend, and how that hurts you. And you can feel what it's like to get centered and peaceful, and how that empowers you.

The more you listen to your body's wisdom, the stronger you get.

A FEW HOURS AFTER my mom cried and told me that she wished I wanted to spend time with her, I took an evening walk on the beach alone. The sand was still warm, but I could feel it cooling quickly. Soon the colors faded from the sky and the ocean turned black. For a long time, I stared out into the darkness. Then to my own surprise, I started to speak.

"Listen," I said. "Just listen. I am angry. I am so angry! Nothing is going the way it is supposed to. I'm working so freaking hard, but somehow it's not enough. My mom acts like I'm supposed to be Super Daughter Mind Reader or something . . ."

I trailed off, then paused and drew a deep breath: "But that's not actually what I want to talk about right now." Raising my voice to a shout, I yelled, "Listen! Here's what I want. I want to get back together with Harley! I've been pretending like that isn't true, but what the hell, it is. Even if it's stupid."

I spoke as though I was on a telephone line with a bad connection: "Are you *getting* this? Are you *hearing* me? This is my plan for my life. And I would like you to start cooperating already!"

It occurred to me that I was praying, though not in a way I'd ever prayed before. All the truths I'd trapped inside came rushing out in raw, radical honesty.

It also occurred to me that I sounded like a crazy person. Then it dawned on me that I *was* a crazy person. Unexpectedly, I heard myself giggle, then laugh, then sob. Hadn't I received every possible indication that my plan for my life wasn't working? Hadn't I been sick enough, tired enough, and heartbroken enough?

Save for the sound of the waves, everything was quiet. I took a few deep breaths, considering whether I ought to feel bad about screaming at God. I didn't feel ashamed, though. I felt as though I'd been gathered up into a pocket of peacefulness by some unseen hand. It felt like sitting with Raymond, only even more profound.

I sensed an incredibly kind Presence, at once deeply familiar and entirely fathomless. The Presence and I sat quietly together for a while. It could have been twenty minutes, or it could have been two hours. All I wanted was to be exactly where I was.

And then the Presence spoke to me. It didn't use words, but in the language of feeling, I heard,

> Your hurt and anger are not too much for me. You can pour all of those emotions out and it will not deplete me one bit. You do not owe me superhuman strength. In fact, I don't need you to do a damn thing for me. I am just here, with you and for you.
>
> I know that you want to get back together with Harley. I will just say this, ever so gently: I have something else in store for you. It's going to be beautiful, sweetheart. Trust me on this one. It's going to be so freaking beautiful.

I felt these truths in my body. They felt like expansion, like the vast ocean before me. It was so interesting: they were truths that my ego did not want to hear, and yet they felt deeply right in my soul.

That night I felt the same kind of mysterious certainty I experienced years later, when Raymond passed away. Though I'd long since moved away from L'Arche by then, I knew the precise moment of his death. I'd been going about my usual evening routine, just stepping out of a bathtub, when suddenly I felt a deep sense of peace and freedom. I actually looked around the room, half expecting to see my old friend there with me.

I knew that it was Raymond. I knew that he was home. I knew that his spirit was free, that his wholeheartedness had reached into majesty. I was stunned by the strength of it, but on a deeper level, I was not surprised. If he had taught me anything, it was that when we risk reaching out, something eternal reaches back to us.

THAT PROFOUND EXPERIENCE REMINDED me to trust my inner knowing. It also reminded me to connect with my true self, the part of me that will endure when I die.

When we're unhappy and in deep emotional pain, it's time to stop compulsively caretaking other people and start paying attention to our own deep truth. It's time to take a look and ask, *Where am I neglecting or hurting myself?*

That's not to say that other people can't abuse or neglect us. They can, and they do. And when we recognize destructive patterns, we need to give ourselves space to mourn and rage. (It isn't right! It isn't fair! I hate this! It shouldn't be this way!)

But when the shock wears off and the dust settles, the question becomes, What is our responsibility going forward? It's not our responsibility to control or change others, but it is our responsibility to take care of ourselves. How can we take care of ourselves in this place or with this person? When there is danger, how will we protect ourselves?

Back when I lived at L'Arche, I was an expert at caring for others. I cared for my housemates, my friends, and my family whenever they needed me. Yet I was only a beginner at caring for myself—the only person I owed caregiving in the first place.

So what does it look like to turn that corner on caring for yourself? When the old addictions tempt you, how do you find the courage to create something new? Where do you begin?

Frankly, I'm still figuring it out. But I'll offer you an embodiment exercise that has helped me a great deal.

THE NO-OWE INVITATION

Play "You're Getting Warmer, You're Getting Colder"

As recovering perfectionists and people-pleasers, we tend to live in our heads. We have an innate mistrust of our physical responses. But what if our best decisions aren't made by endless rationalizations and explanations? What if our next right step is as close as our breath, our skin, our body?

On the physical level, we know what's right for us in any given moment. Our bodies are a fantastic source of information, yet so often we tune them out and ignore them. We spend a lot of time and energy pushing down our truths, and that drains us.

How can we regain strength and practice trusting our bodies? This exercise is a simple yet powerful way to do just that.

Harvard-trained sociologist, coach, and author Martha Beck says that life is like a childhood game of "You're getting warmer, you're getting colder." The great thing about this game is that you don't actually need to know what you're looking for in order to win. You just need to pay attention to the feedback you're getting from the other person, who tells you whether you're closer to or farther away from the object. You win by shifting direction until you get warmer and warmer and you're right on top of the object.

So how do we play this game in our real lives? It's straightforward, though not necessarily easy. We get in tune with our physical responses to different choices and activities in our lives, and we learn to trust those physical responses more than our mind-based explanations. As a coach, I help clients do this using a version of Martha Beck's methodology, which she calls the Body Compass. (Martha Beck writes about this concept at length in her books *Finding Your Own North Star*, *Steering by Starlight*, and *Finding Your Way in a Wild New World*, all of which are excellent.)

Often it's easier to start with the negative (that is, the colder) than the positive (the warmer). Typically, when I ask people what they want, they begin by telling me all the things they don't want. So begin by thinking of a situation that you know was 100 percent wrong for you.

For example, here's a situation that feels very wrong for me, personally: "I'm sitting in a high-school math class, next to this so-called friend who tries to control me." If I picture myself there, my physical body responds. My throat gets tight, my shoulders cave in, and my stomach sinks. I call it the "Trapped in Prison" feeling. That's my "colder."

Conversely, if I picture myself doing ballet, or figure skating to my favorite song, or traveling with my closest friends, or cuddling with my husband, I feel light, expansive, and happy. A smile comes to my face. I call it the "Free as a Bird" feeling. That's my "warmer."

Your invitation is to start noticing your physical responses to the activities, environments, and people in your life. Do not go by what you think about them. Go with how your physical body responds.

Know that you may need to break down your more complex experiences because certain elements may be warmer, while others are colder. For example, you may love spending time with your coworkers but not love the work you're doing together, or vice versa. There are nuances to this process.

For the next week, be an observer of your own experience. Be a scientist. What is it like to be you? When you go to your office, how do you feel? When you get dressed for the party, how do you feel? Are you getting warmer or colder?

Also notice how as you receive the clear signals from your body, your mind will jump in and tell you all the reasons why you "shouldn't" feel that way. This is a great time to revisit the exercises on questioning your thoughts, judgments, and limiting beliefs.

7

You Don't Owe Anyone

Your Compliance

In the family trance . . . the family is the unifying center
that forces a constricted identification or role upon the
family members. To be in the trance is to be so completely
identified with one's role in the family, that important
aspects of one's own personal experiences remain
unconscious. The trance is ultimately the family demanding
compliance rather than authenticity . . . and no small
vulnerable child has the ability to say 'No' to this. . . . The
child scrambles for scraps of safety and belongingness in
the only way offered . . . and pays for it by relinquishing
authenticity.

—John Firman and Ann Gila, *The Primal Wound*

IF YOU'RE OVERCOMMITTED AND overcompliant—stressed out
by saying yes to too many people and too many plans—then here's an
idea for you. It comes from author Derek Sivers, and it has saved me
so much time, money, and energy. When you're faced with a decision,
ask yourself this simple question:

Is this a hell yeah for me? If not, then your answer is no. Those are your choices—either hell yeah or no thanks.

Granted, this line of reasoning doesn't apply to every situation. As Derek Sivers notes, when you're just starting out in your career, it makes sense to say yes to every opportunity to learn. But hell yeah or no is a helpful framework when you've either gained significant expertise or reached capacity in a given area.

Ask yourself, What is really and truly a hell yeah for me? What have I been pretending to say a wholehearted yes to, when in reality the most I can muster is a maybe? What if I let the maybe go?

Maybes are mostly dishonest nos, so they rob us of our energy. Letting go of maybe is terrifying. But it's also liberating.

For example, you might realize that some of the events on your calendar for the next month are not true yeses for you in this season. So let them go. By which I mean RSVP and then feel waves of false guilt. You'll probably hear old judgmental tapes play in your mind: "But you should want to do that! Everyone else wants to do that! What kind of person are you?"

Chances are, you'll feel pretty darn uncomfortable for a couple minutes. Your old self-concept as the Yes Person will die a little bit, and your ego will freak out. You'll think that you should stay in your old yes box because this change—however positive—is just too hard.

But the good news is, the discomfort will fade eventually. And while you're still feeling guilty, you can use one of my favorite tricks from the book *Boundaries*: Rejoice in the guilty feelings. See them as a sign of progress. Actually cheer yourself on for feeling so bad!

To quote from *Boundaries*, "In a funny way . . . activating the hostile conscience is a sign of spiritual growth. . . . If the conscience were silent and providing no 'how could you?' guilt-inducing messages, it might mean you were remaining enslaved to the internal parent. That's why we encourage you to rejoice in the guilt. It means you are moving ahead."

The more you practice connecting to your deeper truth, the easier it gets. And when the discomfort fades, you'll be left with the sweetness of living in integrity. You'll enjoy the freedom that comes when you're not divided against yourself. You'll realize that you don't owe anyone your compliance.

Believe me, I know it's bittersweet to let go of the person you thought you were, the person who said yes to everyone and everything. It takes faith to trust that you will be loved even when you set boundaries.

———

THAT NIGHT ON THE beach with the Presence changed me. I had a glimpse into another reality, one in which I didn't need to hustle and hurt myself in order to feel loved. You'd think this would have made my life better—and in the long run, it certainly did. But in the short term, it wreaked havoc.

The thing about the Presence is that you can't lie to yourself and still stay connected to it. So when you have an encounter like that and then continue breaking yourself apart in order to please others, it hurts even more because you know that there's a better way. As I went back to my usual routine of martyrdom at L'Arche, I felt the pain even more acutely. I began to see the dysfunctional dynamics I'd created with my obsessive self-sacrifice. I began to feel physically and emotionally awful when I refused to protect my own energy. And I began to recognize that certain people took advantage of my constant compliance.

One Saturday afternoon at L'Arche, I was about thirty seconds away from heading upstairs to take a nap when my housemate and direct supervisor Becca bounced into the kitchen and smiled at me. My heart fell at the sight of her.

Becca and I got along when we first met—we both liked watching *Flight of the Conchords* and filling out *Washington Post* crossword puzzles—but our dynamic changed after she came down with a prolonged, unpredictable illness. The rest of our household scrambled to cover her routines, and as weeks went by, I felt our collective frustration and exhaustion mount.

Plus, my parents were as exhausted as I was, if not more so. Willie had graduated from his special-needs school at age twenty-one, but with his behavioral issues, he had nowhere to go after that. He spent his days at home, moving through detailed lists of chores, math worksheets, and exercise reps. Mom and Dad rearranged their work hours to trade off supervising him, and the situation wore on everyone. They were tired and I was tired. The sight of anyone who wasn't tired rankled.

Even so, I forced a smile onto my face as Becca entered the kitchen. I didn't want our new team member Ike picking up on the tension. I wanted Ike to see how good community life could be, and also, I really didn't want him to leave. If any of our new assistants jumped ship, we'd have a hard time covering all of the caregiving time.

"Hey, Caroline!" Becca chirped. "You're away now, right?"

"Um, right," I said. Privately, I thought, *Why are you asking? You already know that my time away starts now because you write the schedules! At least you still do that; we're the ones doing your damn laundry.* In an attempt to distract us both from the smoldering anger I felt, I chirped, "Cute skirt!"

"Thanks!" she said. "It is fun, isn't it?" I nodded. Becca did look cute. She looked like she'd slept in and taken her time getting dressed and putting on lip gloss. On the other hand, I looked like I'd rolled out of bed in yoga pants and pushed myself through eight hours of caregiving. Becca did a little twirl to show off the skirt, and I felt the pit of fury in my stomach ignite. *So now you're well enough to twirl and not get dizzy, but not well enough to do routines?*

As it turned out, she was well enough for more than that. "My friend from Catholic U is having this party tonight," she said. "Could you give me a ride there? The house van is free; I already checked. It shouldn't take long. Could you just drop me off?"

I took a beat, swallowed a sip of water, and felt my stomach turn into an inferno. Did she actually expect me to drive her to a party across town? I met her open-wide-innocent eyes and saw that the answer was yes, she really did. Unlike me, Becca had no qualms about asking for what she wanted. She also didn't hesitate to break an etiquette rule that my mother had drilled into me from an early age: "Never ask someone for a favor in front of someone else. It's unfair to pressure them that way."

Unfair is right, I thought. I was so tired. I had nothing left to give. I opened my mouth to say—*Sorry, I really need to rest*—but an invisible hand stopped me. I couldn't understand exactly why that hand encircled my throat, why telling the truth felt taboo. All I knew was that the hand had been with me all my life, and it was very strong. It was stronger than fatigue, anger, and common sense.

Every fiber of my being was shouting, *No, you cannot say yes to Becca, not this time*. Every fiber, that is, except the ones that were saying, *But Caroline, you have to show Ike how we care for each other in community! You have to be like Jesus! Like your mom says, Jesus let himself be nailed to the cross. So surely you can do this, right?*

With that thought, one word slipped out: "OK."

I wanted to take it back as soon as I'd spoken, but it was too late. Becca and Ike were both smiling.

"Wow," Ike said. "You guys really look out for each other around here."

"I know, right?" Becca agreed.

"Just let me use the bathroom first," I muttered, ducking around the corner and locking the wide, wheelchair-accessible door. Bracing my hands on either side of the white porcelain sink, I looked at my face in the mirror and saw desperation. *You can still say no*, an inner voice whispered. *She can take a bus or the metro. You don't have to do this to yourself.*

But by then, I'd been ignoring my truth so often that it was almost automatic. What was one more sacrifice, one more override of what I knew deep down?

I shook myself and whispered, fiercely, "Just do it. Just get it *done*."

But as Becca and I walked down the wrought-iron stairs and our footsteps crunched across the gravel driveway, I felt my usual control slipping. When I turned the key in the van's ignition, a caged, desperate feeling arose. Becca tried to talk to me, but I couldn't manage more than monosyllables in response: "Yeah." "This turn?" I was shut down to the point of being rude, and the scariest part was that I didn't care.

There was an accident on Michigan Avenue, and cars were stopped in both directions. Our van crept forward. I pressed my foot down again and again in the maddening repetition unique to traffic jams: gas, brake, gas, brake. Every moment that I did not scream or cry or hyperventilate took physical effort. The "quick" drive to the party took us more than an hour.

"Wow, this is crazy traffic," Becca said.

I didn't say a word. I wanted to kill her, but I wanted to kill myself more.

THIS BRINGS US TO the contradiction inherent in people-pleasing. We do it because we want to be good and kind, and we want other people to see us as such. Yet when we throw our own needs under the bus in order to please others, we become the opposite of what we wish to be. We become tense, furious, and most of all, resentful.

When we have no compassion for ourselves, we have no real compassion to give to others either. In *Rising Strong*, Brené Brown observed, "Compassionate people ask for what they need. They say no when they need to, and when they say yes, they mean it. They're compassionate because their boundaries keep them out of resentment."

This is such a key principle. When we do not have healthy boundaries and do not take care of ourselves, we cannot help but be resentful! We cannot help but see others as persecutors, hounding us for our compliance. We cast ourselves as their victims, but in truth, we are the victims of our own poor boundaries.

Sure, Becca's request for a ride wasn't fair, but she didn't make me get into the van that day. That was a choice that I made in order to avoid the guilt I would have felt if I had said no. But instead I ended up feeling guilty for resenting her.

In my experience, the quickest way to resent someone is to promise them more than I can give with integrity. And the quickest way to feel free and easy around them is to maintain healthy boundaries.

As Elizabeth Gilbert wrote, "Until you learn how to hold appropriate boundaries, and stand in integrity, and speak your truth, you will never have a relaxed moment in your life. You will live like a fugitive, always on the run, always hiding, always afraid of being exposed. A heart without healthy and appropriate boundaries can only suffer in a constant state of anxiety and defense—vigilant against the next attack, helpless against other people's will."

That's how I felt in those early days at L'Arche—helpless against other people's wills. Back then, it was hard for me to realize that I didn't owe anyone my compliance.

WHEN AT LAST I pulled up to Becca's friends' building, she opened the passenger door quickly, saying, "Thank you for the ride!" Her tone was on tiptoes. Wisely, she did not ask me to come back and pick her up.

As soon as Becca shut the passenger door, I started crying hysterically. All of the emotion I'd pushed down was coming up; I tasted bile in my mouth. In between gasps, I shouted myself hoarse. "This is not OK. I am not OK!"

I was not OK. It was true, but I didn't know how to fix it. I didn't know what to do except to carry on working hard. So when Becca moved out a few weeks later and I was asked to assume her supervisory role, I said yes. This meant that I'd shoulder more responsibilities, including scheduling routine one-on-one monthly meetings with each assistant on our team. Ruefully, I thought, *Well, I guess there's no more avoiding Jonathan now.*

Jonathan was an assistant who had moved into our L'Arche home the same week I was away at the beach with my family. He had served as an assistant several years before I'd arrived, so the first time I'd seen his face had been on the cover of a L'Arche brochure. Upon meeting Jonathan in person, I found him as handsome and inscrutable as his picture. He gave the impression of tremendous intelligence and self-command.

But when I tried to chat and be friendly, Jonathan didn't meet my gaze. He answered my enthusiastic queries with swift monosyllables. At first, I felt my insides shrink with humiliation. But soon the belief that he didn't like me actually freed me to be myself with him. I'd never capture his interest, so why bother trying? I had plenty to keep me busy with my new role, anyway.

So what if my palm tingled when we slapped high-fives after completing an evening routine? So what if I secretly looked forward to that split second when our hands met? It was nothing because it could never be anything. The shingles scar below my heart still stung when I grew overtired, and that was all the reminder I needed. I knew exactly how much it cost to take a chance on a crush.

I resolved to simply be grateful that Jonathan had come back to L'Arche. He was rational where most of us were idealistic, and thus he was both a fish out of water and exactly what we needed. In his first week back at L'Arche, he swapped out all of the low-watt light bulbs so the house was literally brighter than before. The rest of us had simply accepted the darkness.

ON THE WINTER DAY when Jonathan and I were scheduled for our first one-on-one meeting, I ran a brush through my hair and straightened my fitted gray sweater. I picked up a chain with two tiny silver keys on it, a gift from my grandfather after my grandmother's funeral. The twin keys had been tucked in the back of a velvet-lined jewelry box, and no one had known what they'd unlocked. They symbolized my hope of finding a "match," and I felt a touch of self-recrimination as I clomped down the stairs to meet Jonathan. *Why are you wasting time looking nice for this?* I thought. *You'd have been better off writing a list of topics to discuss. This guy is more taciturn than Mr. Darcy.*

"Hey, how are you?" I asked Jonathan, who was waiting by the back door, on time as usual.

"Doing well. How are you?" he replied, nodding his head and giving me a half-smile.

That hint of positive regard made me blush, so I looked down at my scuffed boots as I said, "I'm quite all right, thank you. Well, then. Shall we go?" Mentally, I scolded myself: *God, Caroline, enough with the formal speech! You are not a character in a Charlotte Brontë novel!*

As Jonathan held the door open for me, a rush of icy-cold air hit. "Oh! It's colder than I thought," I said, shivering involuntarily as we stepped out into the back alley.

I felt rather than saw Jonathan look over at me. He wore only a lightweight black fleece jacket over his trademark plain white T-shirt, but he didn't seem to feel the cold. Yet there was a hint of protective concern in his tone as he asked, "Do you need to go back?"

"No, thanks. It's not great, but I'm always cold anyway. Um. You probably already know that. I'm the one who's always punching up the thermostat when you turn it down. Guilty as charged." My inner critic barked, *Girl, stop babbling!*

"How about Starbucks?" he asked.

"Perfect." It was only a block away, so we wouldn't have far to walk.

He held the door for me again when we reached Starbucks. Jonathan was from Alabama, and while he didn't have an accent, he did have the traditionally southern sense of courtesy. As we entered, I breathed an involuntary sigh of relief. The heat was blasting, and I loved the heady scent of roasting coffee in the air.

"How about you pick the table and I order? It's on L'Arche as usual," I said.

"I'll have a hot chocolate, please. No whipped cream."

I brought back our drinks and took a sip of my coffee. "Oh, this is exactly what I needed today. How's your hot chocolate?"

"It's OK," he said. "Would you like to try it?"

"Seriously?" I asked, raising my eyebrows and calling his bluff. In our house, everyone knew that Jonathan didn't share food.

"Seriously," he said, sliding the hot to-go cup across the checkerboard tabletop to me.

"Well, OK then," I smiled, delighted to be an exception to the rule. Taking a small sip, I exclaimed, "Oh, wow. Yum."

"It's OK, I guess," he said. "But the hot chocolate at Caribou is better. Theirs is the best one that I've tasted."

"Oh, then it must be really good." Suddenly, I felt braver, almost flirtatious. "Well, maybe we can do our meeting there next month. You know, do a taste test."

"Sure," he said, and we both smiled and looked down. Then we started talking about the core members' care and the weekly schedule and even which books we'd been reading, and I forgot to be nervous. I had the lingering taste of rich chocolate in my mouth, sweet as the realization that this meeting wasn't going so badly after all.

During a brief lull in our conversation, "The Chipmunk Song (Christmas Don't Be Late)" came on over the store speakers. I didn't recognize it at first. But as the chipmunks' tinny voices rang out, Jonathan joined them in a pitch-perfect impression.

I started giggling, and he hammed it up even more. By the time he sang the line about wanting a hula hoop, I was doubled over in my chair, laughing so hard that I could barely breathe. When the song ended, I straightened up and said, "Oh my God. That was . . . perfect. No matter what happens now, I can die happy."

Jonathan just grinned back at me.

⟋

JONATHAN AND I DID go to Caribou Coffee for hot chocolate at our next meeting. We also started trading our favorite books and staying up late to talk after the core members had gone to bed. Though I enjoyed our conversations, losing sleep was possibly not the best choice I could have made during flu season. Soon I found myself on the phone with my childhood friend Eva, trying to get out of our dinner plans.

"Eva, I'm so sorry," I said, holding my pounding head in one hand and my cell phone in the other. "I just don't think I can make it tonight. I feel super tired."

"Car, c'mon, you've got to come!" As usual, Eva was not letting me off the hook. "You know Mandy came all the way here to meet up with us!"

I nodded; this was true. Our friend Mandy and her husband, Allen, had flown in to DC for the weekend. How could I possibly bail?

"But Eva, I feel like total crap. Like, sick. I feel awful."

"Just rest now so you'll feel better for later. We're going to Lauriol Plaza, OK? We'll get margaritas and it will be great."

The thought of tequila and Mexican food made my stomach roll. It was Becca and the house van all over again; before I knew it, I'd agreed to the plan I'd called to cancel. Flinging the phone down in angry defeat, I slid under the covers and closed my eyes.

Just before I lost consciousness, I thought back to all the times that I'd let Eva talk me into doing what she wanted. I thought back to all the times she'd been late to meet me over the last year and a half, how I'd waited around and swallowed my frustration at various coffee shops. Had I ever really set a boundary on my time or said no to her? Did I always act like I owed her my compliance? I fell asleep before I figured it out.

That night, Eva's glee at my appearance gave me a brief boost—"Yay, you made it!"—but by the time we met Mandy and Allen at the overcrowded restaurant bar, I could barely force myself to follow the conversation, much less contribute to it. Just a few minutes after we'd arrived, I broke in: "Guys, I'm so sorry, but I seriously don't feel well. I really need to get some air."

The air outside was frigid, but I tore off my coat and scarf. Standing made my head spin, so I wobbled over to a bus shelter, sinking onto the hard, gray bench. *Guess I must have a temperature*, I thought, *because the cold air feels amazing on my face. I wonder if this is what it's like for Jonathan when the weather is hot and he stands in the freezer at home.*

Home . . . I would have given anything to be home. When Allen came outside, though, I tried to pull myself together.

"Hey, Mandy sent me out to check on you. Are you OK?" he asked.

"I'm . . . well . . . I'm not sure," I hedged. It was the best I could do. "I just can't go back. I can't breathe in there, it's too hot. I need to stay out here."

"OK," he said. An awkward silence descended. Then he said, "Well, hope you feel better," and went back inside.

I waited alone for some time longer. As the minutes passed, it dawned on me: *Mandy is not coming out. Eva is not coming out either. I couldn't be who she wanted me to be tonight. I'm on my own.*

THE GREAT THING ABOUT saying yes when you mean no is that you get to avoid finding out who loves you for you and who loves you for your compliance. But the terrible thing about being a Yes Person is that you cannot avoid this reckoning forever. Eventually, you will falter. You will get tired; you will get sick. You will not be able to come through for your people. And it is both terrifying and instructive to see how they respond when that happens.

That's what I discovered when I sat on the bus-shelter bench outside the restaurant that night. I tried to read the bus schedule, but the tiny letters blurred and the L2 was never on time anyway. Craning my neck forward, I prayed to see the bright lights of a bus. Nothing.

What next? Pulling my cell phone from my purse, I called the L'Arche house number, and Jonathan picked up.

"Hello?"

"Oh, hi, Jonathan. It's me. It's Caroline. Um." I didn't want to admit weakness in front of him, but there was no getting around it. "I'm at Lauriol Plaza. I was supposed to have dinner with friends, but I feel bad. Sick. I don't think I can walk home. I know you're on routine, but is there anyone else around who isn't? And maybe . . . they could come and pick me up?" Saying this caused me no small amount of shame. Perhaps I'd become like Becca, begging rides from people who were already exhausted.

"I'm sorry to hear that. Hang on, let me check if anyone is around," Jonathan said.

After a pause, he was back. "Sorry, I can't find anyone. It's Saturday night." He sounded genuinely distressed.

"I'd come right away if I could," he said, and I knew he meant it. "But Raymond's already in bed, and with the certification issue . . ."

"I get it, totally, you have to stay," I said, swallowing hard against the bile rising in my throat. Due to DC Medicaid regulations, we had to have two certified assistants present with the core members at the home at all times.

A wave of embarrassment crested over me along with the desire to vomit, and I rushed to say, "Sorry to bother you. I'll figure something out."

Just then, an L2 bus came into view. "It's an L2! Thank God," I said as I got off the phone.

"OK, good," he said. "Be safe. I'll look for you soon."

Somehow I boarded the bus and walked the remaining block home from the bus stop, praying that I wouldn't puke in the street. Somehow I unlocked the back door, but my willpower took me no further than a nearby table, where I sat and lay my head down. The Ben Lee song "Gamble Everything for Love" played from the kitchen CD player, and one of our housemates, Pedro, started chatting to me.

When Jonathan came in, he took one look at me and said to Pedro, "Para Carolina, silencio, por favor." Pedro obeyed. It was the first time I'd ever heard Jonathan speak Spanish, the first time I'd ever heard him use the Hispanic version of my name. *Car-o-leen-a*, I thought. *So pretty. I like how it sounds when he says it. Like music.*

"How do you feel?" Jonathan asked.

I groaned. "Not good."

"You don't look like yourself. Here, I'll get you some water," he said, pouring a glass and placing it in front of me. "Whatever it is, staying hydrated will help. Are you hungry at all?"

"Maybe. I'm not sure I can eat, though."

"How about toast?"

Jonathan popped bread into the toaster, then went to check on the core members. "Don't get up, I'll be right back," he said, and I believed him. Laying my head back down on my hands, I realized that this wasn't the first time Jonathan had taken care of me. When he saw me reach for a banana, he took the peanut butter out of the cupboard and handed it over; when he saw me shiver, he brought me a blanket. Once he'd even tucked it over my shoulders.

True to his word, Jonathan brought over a piece of perfectly browned toast a moment later. I sipped water and took a few bites, which gave me the boost I needed to trudge up the stairs and throw up for the rest of the night.

The next afternoon, I woke to a gentle knock on my door. Earlier Eva had texted and Mandy had come to visit, but though I appreciated their efforts, I could barely muster energy to talk. I'd been sleeping for most of the day.

When I called, "Come in!" Jonathan appeared with a tray of food.

All at once, I became aware of my hastily chosen pajamas. In a haze of fever, I'd donned a bulky, unflattering gray sweatshirt from a WCG youth retreat with *Wonderland Conference Center* printed on the chest. Yet the flame of self-consciousness flickered only momentarily; I was too exhausted to sustain it.

"Oh, wow, thank you for bringing food," I said. "It's a pretty rough stomach flu—I don't recommend it. Anyway, thank you for being so kind to me last night."

"Of course," he said.

Jonathan had brought me a tray of toast and soup, and he'd included a stick of mint gum too.

"The gum is a nice touch."

"Thanks," he replied. "When you're sick, it's hard to get up and brush your teeth."

"You thought of everything," I said. Somehow I wasn't embarrassed about needing help anymore. Instead, I was touched by how he'd cared for me.

"You're welcome." He paused, lingering for a beat. His brown eyes were dark, and before he turned away, I thought I saw a flash of a fierce kind of tenderness.

He didn't say anything romantic, and I didn't let myself believe that he had feelings for me. But a few mornings later, I stumbled out of bed and stepped on a piece of paper lying on the rug just under my door. It was a torn sheet from our house's scrap-paper bin. On one side, I saw part of a handout from a medication training course with instructions on how to insert a rectal suppository. The other side of the paper bore Jonathan's trademark scrawl: *CF, go back to bed! I'm up anyway and will do this AM.—JM.*

He'd never said a romantic word to me, but he'd given me permission to rest. He would take care of the morning routine, and I could go back to bed. Bed! Crawling back under the covers, I slipped the note under my pillow. Before sleep overtook me, I thought, *Even if he doesn't like me as more than a friend, this is still the best love letter I've ever received. Thank you, thank you, thank you.*

THE SILVER LINING OF being sick and tired at L'Arche was that it took me out of my usual game. Illness gave me space to reflect on my relationships, and I sensed a seed of awareness taking root: *The way I've been doing relationships isn't working anymore. I know how to give even when I'm super depleted, but I'm not comfortable letting myself receive. I feel shy around Jonathan ever since he took care of me. Actually, I've been avoiding him. And I'm mad at Eva and Mandy about what happened when we went out, but I'm more mad at myself. I keep ignoring my health and well-being in order to please others. How do I stop doing that?*

I needed a new way of thinking about what it meant to be a giver. I needed to start from scratch and redefine the term. Was there a way to give to others without disregarding myself?

If you've been asking the same question, you'll be relieved to hear that the answer is yes.

Years after I left L'Arche, I discovered a great book called *Give and Take* in which author Adam Grant states that there are two different types of Givers. The first and most successful type gives while guarding personal limits. Grant calls them the "Otherish Givers." They set healthy boundaries, holding self-interest and other-interest simultaneously. For them, it's not self or others—it's self *and* others.

By contrast, the second and least-successful type gives to the point of exhaustion. Grant calls them the "Selfless Givers." They have trouble saying no to anyone. As a result, they are always, always tired.

I used to be one of them, of course. I used to think that if I didn't give away every ounce of energy to others, I was being selfish. Often we equate being a Giver solely with selflessness, with being depleted. But there is another way. In order to find it, we must be willing to go into new territory. We must step off the familiar path of people-pleasing and actually honor our personal limits.

What does this look like in real life? In *Give and Take*, Grant gives the example of a college professor who felt overwhelmed by student requests for guidance and support. The professor wanted to help, but he felt hounded by the constant requests. The solution was to set specific office hours and limit student consultations to those times. That might sound simple, but how many times have you felt beleaguered by your email or your phone? And how many times have you set limits on your own availability? Few people question the pervasive premise that we must be constantly available to others.

The thought of setting limits feels taboo; we sense ostracism lurking, ready to pounce the moment we stop our usual patterns. Often our first response is fear: *What if they hate me?*

When such a fearful question arises, question its premise. Instead of asking, *What if they hate me?* question the origin of that idea. *Wait a minute, where is this coming from, this belief that I need to rescue others and abandon myself? Is this something I'd want to pass on to someone I love? Why, exactly, do I believe that I owe other people my compliance?*

When I questioned the premise recently, I expected to bump up against my brother's diagnosis or perhaps a memory from the WCG. But when I let myself sit with the question and follow the energy back, it took me to the first day of kindergarten.

Before Dad and I left the house, Mom gave me a hug and said, "Cari, I wish I could go with you to school, but listen; I have something important to tell you. It's the same thing that my mother told me on my first day of school." She paused, smiling at the memory, then continued: "If you want to make a friend, look for a girl who seems even more scared and upset than you. Then introduce yourself to her and be really nice to her. She'll be so happy about it that she'll be your friend. Can you do that? Can you be brave?"

I nodded, and Mom beamed. "Good. Now, you have a good day."

But as Dad and I got out of the car and walked up to the elementary school, I didn't feel brave at all. I tried to pretend, but it was hard. When the classroom aide asked me to smile for a picture, I tried to mask the naked fear. Yet with a gentle nudge from Dad, I followed Mom's instructions. Swallowing hard so that I wouldn't cry, I walked up to a sobbing girl who looked a lot like me except with shorter, wavier hair.

"Hi, my name is Caroline," I said, shyly. "What's your name?"

"Jen," she mumbled. "But I don't wanna go to school! I want my mommy!" Her Bambi-brown eyes were red from crying.

"Um . . . we can go in together." I paused, then risked it: "Maybe . . . do you want to be friends?"

"Really?" she said, her eyes brightening. "OK."

My mom was right, it was just that easy. It was easy to make a friend, to rescue somebody who was drowning even though I wasn't so sure that I could swim.

The lesson I learned about friendship—passed down with good intentions from grandmother to mother to daughter—was based on a one-down model. You're upset, and I help you feel better, regardless of how I feel. I will give you what you want and need, and in return, you will like me. I will connect with you by pushing down my own feelings and helping you with yours.

But what if instead I'd heard that it was OK to feel afraid? *Go find someone who feels scared, and then tell her that you're afraid too.* Or what if I'd heard an encouragement to trust my intuition? *Go toward someone who seems kind, someone who you have a feeling could be a good friend.*

That's what I'm practicing nowadays: Feeling the feelings, allowing myself the full human experience, and connecting with other humans. Saying yes or no based on what feels right to me, not because I owe anyone my compliance. Being strong in a different way—strong enough to take care of my own heart.

THE NO-OWE INVITATION

Follow the Energy Back

Following the energy back is a wonderful, spiritual psychology exercise with its roots in Gestalt psychology. The basic principle of Gestalt is "the whole of anything is greater than its parts." It's focused on helping people gain awareness and connect with their actual, felt experience (as opposed to their beliefs and ideas about their experience). I first learned this exercise from the good people at The Clearing and have modified it based on my own work with clients. Use this exercise the next time you feel disproportionately upset by anything in your life.

Note that this exercise is deep, emotional-level work, so often it's best to learn this process with a trusted, experienced facilitator, such as a coach or counselor. That said, you also have all the resources that you need to heal within you, so I offer this exercise to you trusting that you will use it in a way that's right for you. All you need is a quiet, private space, with two separate places to sit down.

Begin by getting centered and calm in your loving heart space. As you'll recall, this simply means getting still and connecting to an experience of love within yourself. It might be love for a child, partner, or pet; all that matters is that you activate a feeling of love flowing to and from you. Once you've done that, set a positive intention to heal. (I typically say, "My intention is to heal at the deepest level possible.")

Then, call to mind a situation when you wanted to say no to someone and complied against your better judgment. (If that isn't applicable, pick any situation where you felt very upset—particularly if you thought that your reaction was over the top under the circumstances.) Locate the specific feeling of emotional turbulence that arose in your body at the time. Describe it in detailed physical terms. Write it down: Where does this feeling live in your physical body? Is it sharp or muted, hot or cold, heavy or light? Where else is the discomfort showing up in your body?

For example, you might have a feeling of sadness that's so intense it constricts your throat or a feeling of fear that turns your stomach to an icy pool. You can use metaphor if you'd like, just be sure to focus on a physical sensation rather than a mental-level explanation "I feel like he shouldn't have done that," is a mental-level judgment, not a feeling. You want something along the lines of, "I feel a sharp pain in my stomach."

The first feeling that may come up is anger. If so, that's completely fine; describe it in detail, and then also invite yourself to go a little deeper. What else do you feel? What's the hurt underneath the anger? You'll know you've hit pay dirt when you can find a feeling of hurt, vulnerability, and emotional pain.

Hold that uncomfortable feeling in your body for just a little bit longer. Then ask yourself, "What's the very first time that I can remember feeling this way?"

Follow the energy back to the first time you can remember. Closing your eyes helps; shut out all external stimuli and go inward. You'll probably flip through a few memories before landing on the one that clicks. Be patient. Be still. You're looking for a particular feeling of resonance, a sense of a puzzle piece sliding into place.

Note that this feeling of alignment might not make any sense to your mind. You may not believe that there's any connection between that past moment and this present one. That is perfectly fine; you do not need to understand on the mental level right now. For now, just go with where you feel the energetic connection in your body.

If you're feeling really stuck and can't find that first memory, simply hold the feeling in your body and ask, "How old do I feel right now?" Whatever number pops to mind is the right one.

Once you've identified either a specific memory or a specific age, it's time to do a brief dialogue with your younger self. With your eyes still closed, invite that younger version of yourself into the room with you. Wait until you can picture your past self sitting across from you. When you feel like your younger self has arrived, greet her and thank her for coming. Study her for a moment; observe her responses and posture.

Then, with your eyes still closed, ask her a simple question: "What are you feeling?"

At this point, switch seats. Go and sit down in the space where you envisioned your younger self.

Then answer the question that you just asked as your younger self. Imagine that you are your younger self speaking back to your older self. Use first-person pronouns. Instead of "My younger self feels," say "I feel." Speak in the voice of your younger self.

It might feel strange at first, and that's OK. I invite you to experiment and see what happens. Since you're all the ages that you've ever been, this is just a way to connect with another part of your consciousness; it's a way to access blocked feelings and truths. It's rather like a live-action version of the opposite-hand writing practice that you learned earlier.

Let your younger self say everything that she is feeling. Do not hold back, edit, or censor her. Simply listen to her say whatever she wants to say, holding space for her to have all of her feelings. Maintain an attitude of permission: Here she can be entirely honest. Anything goes.

If she needs more prompts, you may ask more questions: "What's it like to be you?" "What's going on with you?" Fully inhabit your younger self by speaking in a way that she would speak, using language she would use. For example, the grown-up version of you might say, "I understand that when she raised her voice to me, it just shows that she has significant anger issues of her own," whereas the younger version of you would say, "I don't like that she yelled at me! I felt scared!"

Once you have given your younger self plenty of space to share, switch seats again, going back into your grown-up self for a moment. Offer any comfort and reassurance that you want to give your younger self. Then ask your younger self one more question: "What do you need to feel safe and loved?"

Switch seats again and listen closely to the response that arises from within your younger self. Seek out the truest possible answer— often it's the simplest one. Your younger self may say, "I want a hug," or "I want to go home," or "I want my mommy and daddy to be here with me." Just listen.

Then switch seats and go back into your grown-up self, and follow through on the request to the best of your ability. If your younger self needs a hug, wrap your arms around yourself. If your younger self wants you to listen, make a commitment to listen and then honor that by checking in periodically. This is how you build trust with the different parts of yourself and heal the old hurts.

Now you might be wondering, What do I do if my younger self asks for something that I can't give? What if she wants her parents to hold her, and her parents have died?

In that case, you honor the original request without trying to change it—"I hear that you want your parents to hold you"—then offer reassurance and the best of what you have to give in the moment. For example, "They're not here physically right now, but I am. I'm holding you; I'm giving you a hug right now. I love you."

Your younger self is a child, and children need a loving, attentive presence they can trust to come through for them and provide for them. They need reassurance that even though they cannot always get exactly what they want in the form in which they want it, they will not be left to manage their big emotions alone.

Finally, once you've provided for your younger self, you can tell her anything that you want her to know. Often I'll ask my clients, "What do you want your younger self to know? What do you want to tell her?" I am always amazed by the wisdom and love that comes through when I hear clients speak to their younger selves. If possible, record or write down what you say to your younger self so that you can repeat it and reinforce it.

To close the dialogue, thank your younger self for coming to speak with you. Then praise your adult self for having the courage to do this powerful work.

Be very gentle with yourself after doing this exercise. Again, this is deep, emotional-level work, somewhat akin to surgery. You're healing big hurts, and it demands a lot of energy. Drink a lot of water, go for a relaxed walk outside, and take a nap or go to sleep earlier. And praise yourself for a job well done.

8

You Don't Owe Anyone

an Explanation

The most revolutionary thing a woman can do is not explain
herself.
—Glennon Doyle, "I Support Your Right to Share My Rights"

I KNOW A LOT of people who want a different life. Over the years,
I've coached hundreds of them, and though their circumstances
differ, often their fundamental stories are the same.

They want to live somewhere different and do something different. But most of all, they want to *feel* different. They want to feel
happy. Confident. Free. On the same level as other adults rather than
one level down.

Lately I'm getting better at guessing who will create something
new and who won't. I'm noticing three key factors. The first factor is
their ability to do what they say they will do—that is, their integrity.
Do they keep their word to themselves and others?

The second factor is what I refer to as their willingness to dig.
Here I credit the "Monte Cristo" approach, a term coined by Martha Beck. It's a reference to the Alexandre Dumas novel *The Count of*

Monte Cristo, in which hero Edmond Dantes and his fellow prisoner Faria spend years digging a tunnel to escape from prison.

Beck says that when you're imprisoned by a circumstance you're unable to escape at the moment, then you must start digging. Little by little, you must start tunneling a path toward freedom. This isn't the same as the kind of constant pushing that leads to burnout. You don't dig the tunnel in a day. Rather, you take consistent, committed action over time, bit by bit, in the direction of your liberation.

It doesn't matter how impossible it seems or how long you believe the digging will take. You must move what dirt you can.

That brings us to the third key factor: defiance. In order to create a new life for yourself, you need a spark of the rebel in you. You need to be willing to erode and undermine the old in order to make way for the new. Digging the tunnel to freedom is both an act of creation *and* an act of destruction. For those of us who are people-pleasers and perfectionists, the idea of making a mess or ruffling feathers can feel very uncomfortable.

But if we're going to get free from our prisons, then we need to learn to tolerate that discomfort. When we recognize that we're trapped, we must not waste time asking permission to do what is essential for our liberation.

How do you think it would have worked if Edmond Dantes had asked his jailers, "Please, may I dig a tunnel to freedom?" He never would have made it out.

The accusatory voices in our heads are never going to give us permission to leave our old lives. Instead, we'd do well to follow Dantes' example; we'd be wise to connect with a trusted friend and dig together. To work toward a different future, without explaining it to anyone else.

In my experience, this choice tends to come more easily to men, since our patriarchal society assigns them more personal agency. Again, "the most revolutionary thing a woman can do is not explain herself." Not offering explanations, justifications, and rationales is a deeply subversive act for a woman because it implies that she has assumed her own agency and become her own authority.

When you are your own authority, explanations are *not necessary*.

When you are the one in command of your own life, you do not owe anyone an explanation.

—

THERE ARE MOMENTS IN every life that divide time into before and after, being and becoming. When I came to one such crossroads a few months shy of my twenty-fourth birthday, there was no overt drama. I wasn't battling an evil witch or gliding around in a ball gown like the heroines in the Disney movies that Willie watched on repeat. In fact, I was still in my pajamas. I'd spent the better part of a precious day off sequestered in my third-floor bedroom at L'Arche. Though my stomach ached, I didn't dare to venture out for food. I'd resolved not to unlock my door until I had a plan. But no plan was forthcoming. There was only the gentle swish of my monkey slippers as I paced the forest-green carpet and the sound of my one-word prayer: "Help!" Occasionally I'd expand to, "Please, please let me not have ruined everything."

I was in love with Jonathan. Of course I was. However, this was problematic for several reasons. I had a supervisory role in relation to him, and L'Arche's rules were clear: I was not supposed to date an assistant on the team.

Plus, ever since the breakup with Harley a year and a half earlier, I knew just how painful it could be to see an ex every day. I knew how hard it was to move on with no distance to diminish the emotional impact. The case against starting a new relationship seemed ironclad. Yet I couldn't quite get my heart to go along with my head, since—wonder of wonders!—Jonathan loved me too. The night before, we'd kissed for the first time, and the memory of it brought both elation and despair. What if I let our relationship unfold? What if I didn't? I tugged at my brown hair, winding thick strands between my fingers, considering the options. One of my more anxious housemates pulled his graying hairline, and I understood why. Hair was simple and soothing, whereas reality was complex and terrifying.

My stomach felt as twisted up as my hair, guilt and shame swirling together to stifle the stubborn joy. However much I wanted to believe otherwise, falling in love with Jonathan had to be wrong. And if it was wrong, then I had to stop it somehow. Instinctively, my right hand moved from my hairline to my upper left rib cage, grazing the raised shingles scars. I didn't want to risk making another mistake.

WHEN WE'RE SHAMED FOR making mistakes as children, we try really hard to avoid them as adults. When we were little, we were quick learners; we learned to explain ourselves constantly, to prepare an advance justification for every move we made. It was a survival mechanism, and for a time, it served us.

Yet we take that same defensive posture with us into adulthood. Rarely do we believe that "Because I want to" is reason enough. Instead we turn to people-pleasing; we seek a group consensus and offer detailed rationales for our decisions. We feel the need to justify our choices. We can drive loved ones crazy with overexplanations about why we bought that book or decided to take that day off. We believe that we owe the world an explanation.

We think that if we find the right words to help "them" understand, then everything will be all right. Actually, the problem is that we're explaining ourselves and our decisions to "them" in the first place.

That's what I was searching for that day in my room: a blameless narrative, an explanation that would make sense to me and everyone else. After hours of circuitous thought, I felt my empty stomach rumble. The hunger was bad, but the anxiety was worse. I stalked across the room to my small closet, flinging open the door and glaring at the back corner. It didn't look scary—just a few pairs of shoes and my old figure skates—but I knew better. Closets were where I hid when life spun out of control, where I huddled up and hyperventilated.

I didn't step inside, though; recently, carpet beetles had gnawed a small hole in one of the walls and chewed through an old tartan skirt. Though the room had been treated and I'd taped up the gap, I still viewed the space with skepticism. For months now, I'd been unwilling to risk revisiting the dark corners of my closet or my psyche.

I'd been raised on the idea of One True Church and One Right Way, but I couldn't see a clear path out of this situation. So I did what any good Christian girl would do: I leaned over my pile of books and picked up my soft-cover Bible. As I turned the rice-paper-thin pages, I felt for the comfort of my favorite verses and fought to believe that God wasn't furious with me.

When I reread Jesus's words about the sparrows in the book of Matthew, the familiar words eased the tension in my shoulders: "Are not two sparrows sold for a penny? Yet not one of them will fall to the ground outside your Father's care. And even the very hairs of your head are all numbered. So don't be afraid; you are worth more than many sparrows."

Trusting in the God of the sparrow was part of daily life with my housemates with special needs. As a caregiver, I came face-to-face with both physical fragility and spiritual strength. And since our community comprised people of all different faiths, it gave me a glimpse of a God bigger than I'd imagined. It was a God present not in spite of mistakes and frailties but rather within them. For weeks, I'd been feeling a subtle shift toward this idea. It was a sort of spiritual heliotropism, an inward turning like a leaf angling itself toward the light.

I was beginning to wonder if maybe—just maybe—God wasn't judging us after all. Maybe we didn't have to explain our every move and fearfully beg forgiveness. Maybe God had never wanted that from us. Maybe I could trust the feeling I'd had at the beach, the freedom I felt when I realized that the Presence didn't need a damn thing from me, including an explanation. Maybe I didn't have to come up with an elaborate explanation for why I wanted to be with Jonathan. Maybe love was enough.

Yet this fledgling faith warred with my early conditioning; the two battled it out in my bedroom that day. Would I cling to the old concepts or embrace something new? Would I keep viewing the world through perfectionistic lenses, or would I choose more gracious glasses?

"Please help me," I whispered. "I just don't know what to do."

I waited, but nothing came. Dispirited, I put down the Bible. Slinging a rainbow-knitted blanket over my shoulders to block the

February chill, I decided to take a quick break from desperation to read work emails on my laptop.

And so it was that when I begged for help from God, I didn't get a choir of angels or a booming voice telling me what to do. Instead, I got an email from a coworker named Bob.

Bob was one of the older direct-care assistants, a retired businessman in his sixties. He was the kind of guy who would have been friends with my dad: affable, with laugh lines and a cheesy sense of humor. But Bob also had a contemplative side, as evidenced by the email he'd forwarded to me. He wrote something along the lines of, "Hey, Caroline, what you shared at last week's meeting reminded me of this passage, so I felt like I needed to send it your way. Enjoy!"

Below, Bob had included a reflection titled *The Navajo Rug* from Richard Rohr's book *Radical Grace: Daily Meditations*:

In a Navajo rug there is always an imperfection woven into the corner. And interestingly enough, it's where "the Spirit moves in and out of the rug." The pattern is perfect and then there's one part of it that clearly looks like a mistake. The Semite mind, the Eastern mind (which, by the way, Jesus would have been much closer to) understands perfection in precisely that way. Perfection is not the elimination of imperfection. That's our Western either/or, need-to-control thinking. Perfection, rather, is the ability to incorporate imperfection! There's no other way to live: You either incorporate imperfection, or you fall into denial. That's how the Spirit moves in or out of our lives.

As I read the email, I got goosebumps and an almost electrical tingling on my skin. I glanced around, as though I was being watched. One thing I knew for sure: those words were not random. That particular email with that particular quote on this particular day—it was too precise to be called coincidence.

How strange that some unremembered words of mine had prompted Bob to send such a profound passage! How bizarre that my past self had weighed in on my present self's problem through the medium of Bob! And yet, how oddly fitting for the God of the sparrow to speak not though thunder or lightning but rather through a friend.

Spooked and awestruck, with the hairs on my neck standing up, I made a decision. I would gamble on love.

I would do so in an upfront, ethical way; I would meet with my supervisors at L'Arche, and we would figure out a workable solution to the policy issue. Someone else would mentor Jonathan, and soon I would move out of the house to live in my own apartment. And when people would ask me about the decision, I wouldn't defend or justify the choice I'd made. There would be no need to explain the decision to others because I understood it within myself. And for once, that was enough.

AS AN AUTONOMOUS ADULT, you get to do what you want. You are allowed to trust yourself. I know it feels complicated and fraught; I know you have years of programming and conditioning telling you otherwise. But what I'm discovering is that it's as simple as remembering what is true, which is that you are here on earth for just a little while. In light of your mortality, why would you waste time explaining your life to others? Why *wouldn't* you go where the life is, regardless of whether other people "get it"?

In his famous Stanford commencement speech, Steve Jobs said, "Remembering that you are going to die is the best way I know to avoid the trap of thinking you have something to lose. You are already naked. There is no reason not to follow your heart."

You can follow your heart, your gut, and your conscience. You can follow where the Spirit moves, even when it doesn't make sense to others. Sometimes the choice that looks like a "mistake" to someone else is actually the most life-giving for you.

That's how it was for me, at least. Jonathan and I were deeply in love, and our relationship was serious from the start. So when my parents and brother visited DC, I reserved a table for the five of us at a nearby restaurant. I did so picturing a calm, candlelit "meet the parents" meal like the one that Jonathan and I had shared with his parents a few weeks prior. Jonathan's parents had asked thoughtful questions and laughed at my jokes. I'd held Jonathan's hand underneath the table and relaxed a little in light of his family's approval.

As I prepared for the meal with my family, I smoothed the lines of my black-and-white pencil skirt and satin top. I twirled my silver necklace with the Celtic cross charm, humming along with Patti Griffin's song "Heavenly Day." The weather was bright and clear, Jonathan and I were together, and I was happy. And my family had had such a great dinner at L'Arche the night before! Willie had done so well. He'd been his best self, calm and friendly and sweet.

But when Jonathan and I crossed the uneven red-brick sidewalk to meet my family outside the restaurant, Willie had his big noise-canceling headphones on already. That should have told me everything I needed to know about how our meal would go.

As Jonathan and I drew nearer, Willie glanced up at Dad. "I'll be a calm young man," Willie said, an evident edge to his words.

My heart fell. What had gone wrong? I injected cheerfulness into my voice and said, "Hello, family!"

"Hi, Cari!" Mom said, reaching over to give me a hug. "Nice to see you again, Jonathan!"

I turned to greet Willie. Deciding not to risk a hug, I leaned a little closer so that Willie could hear me through his headphones. Taking care to speak gently, I said, "Hi, my favorite brother. How are you, Mr. Willikins?" I used an old nickname in hopes that it would make him smile.

"I'm o-kay," Willie said, with emphasis that signaled, *I'm angry. Don't mess with me.*

Making my voice as soothing as possible, I said, "OK, Willie. We're going to have some dinner. Maybe hamburgers and french fries. It's no big deal."

"No big deal," he echoed.

"And do you know what? I've been dreaming of a wish come . . . hmm, how does that go? Is it a wish come . . . purple?"

I was initiating his favorite game, the one he'd loved since child-hood: the game of the purposeful mistake. He thought it was hilarious when I messed up well-known phrases on purpose.

"No!" Willie said, adamant.

"Is it a wish come ... blue?"

"No!" Willie said again, with the smallest of smiles.

"What is it? Help me out, I can't remember."

"It's a wish come true!" he told me, with a touch of triumph.

"Oh, right, right! I forgot." I said.

Willie laughed, but it was high-pitched, far too forced. *Shit*, I thought.

At dinner, we attempted conversation in fits and starts, with ongoing interruptions from Willie. Eventually Mom handed Willie one of his favorite Richard Scarry cartoon books, and he opened it to a page I'd seen dozens of times before. *Maybe that will help him calm down*, I thought.

"So, Jonathan, your folks just came up from Alabama for a visit?" Mom asked.

"Yes, they did," he replied. "Just for a few days. Mainly to meet Caroline." He gave me a side-smile, and I leaned into him a little bit in acknowledgment.

"They were so nice," I said. "They—"

Willie cut me off, frustrated: "*I'll* read this book *again!*"

"So, Jonathan," Mom began. "Caroline told us that you play guitar and that you worked in live audio before you came to L'Arche, is that right?"

Usually Jonathan was the master of the monosyllable when he met new people, but this time he expanded his answers, telling my parents about his past work. He was trying, and I was touched.

"That's great," Dad said. "So now, what—"

Willie broke in: "Is two plus two *five*?"

"No, Willie," Dad said, with forced humor. "That's bad math!"

"Bad math" was Willie's latest compulsion. When he was stressed, he'd repeat incorrect equations over and over.

"Let's get our orders ready," Mom said. "Willie, a burger with no bun and fries, right? Is that what you want?"

"Yes, I want a burger and french fries!" Willie chirped, using a shrill, pseudocheerful voice.

"OK, we'll order that for you," Mom said.

Just then the waitress rounded the corner, so I resisted the urge to say something about Willie being capable of ordering for himself. After placing my own order, I sank back into my seat and gave Jonathan a wan smile.

As the waitress turned her back, I seized my chance to speak: "Jonathan once ran sound for Alicia Keys!" In the little lull that followed, it occurred to me that I'd just waved Jonathan's accomplishment over our table like a magic wand, as though it had the power to make everything all right. Hadn't I done the same thing with my own accomplishments growing up, with my great grades and good behavior? It was my usual script, just with a different lead character.

"Wow," Mom said. "That sounds exciting. So, remind me again, what does—"

"Is one plus one *four*?" Willie asked, his voice loud in the quiet restaurant.

As we tried to carry on some semblance of conversation, I fidgeted in the banquette seat. When our food finally came, I wolfed down my veggie burger so that we could leave before Willie really lost it. No matter how many times we answered Willie's "bad math" questions, anxiety radiated from his body.

By the time Dad paid for our food, Willie was already on his feet, cramming books into his backpack and dashing out the door. We reached the entryway just in time to see Willie slam his left fist into the wall. I flinched.

"Willie!" Dad said as Willie moved down the block. "You need to take some deep breaths and get calm!"

Willie kept walking, but when Mom turned and waved at me to follow, I found that my legs wouldn't move.

"Hey, mi Carolina," Jonathan said softly as he reached for my hand. "What's going on?"

"I'm sorry," I said. "I'm just sorry about this."

He furrowed his brow in that professorial way I loved, considering, then said, "I don't think you have anything to apologize for."

I thought I owed him an explanation, but what could I say? "I wanted you to see..."

What they're really like, I meant to say, but the irony of my intended words stopped me. The meal we'd shared was typical for my family, as was the bereft feeling that rose up as I watched my parents and brother walk away. My heart ached for my brother, for the pain in him that I didn't understand. My heart ached for our parents, for all the ways in which they'd tried to help Willie, for every difficulty they faced on a daily basis. My heart ached for all of us, trying to connect and missing each other. I wanted to explain them to Jonathan, but they were people, and people do not fit into tidy boxes.

So instead I focused on the feeling of Jonathan's hand in mine, the sense of concern for me that radiated from his body. *Perhaps I don't have to explain,* I thought. *Perhaps I can simply stand in the pain and be seen.*

IT WAS AFTER MIDNIGHT when the last of Jonathan's and my guests left our wedding "rehearsal" party, during which we'd done no rehearsing whatsoever. Technically, it was the morning of our wedding day when I walked the last of our guests to the door of our tiny studio apartment. Brooke had been the first to arrive, and Tam and her partner were the last to leave.

After I closed the door for the last time, I stood in the cramped kitchen of our apartment, trying to summon the energy to wash a pile of chocolate-crusted silverware. I felt the weight of every major life change I'd made in the past few months crashing over me like a wave.

Jonathan rounded the corner, took one look at my deer-in-the-headlights expression, and said, "I'm right here, OK? I'll clean up the kitchen. You start getting ready for bed." Gently, he drew me into his arms. I buried my face in his shoulder, breathing in the usual Speed Stick deodorant scent along with hints of cocoa and vanilla from the chocolate chess pie he'd baked earlier that day.

"Really?" I asked, leaning into him. Accustomed as I was to shouldering responsibility alone, it had not occurred to me that he would offer to help or that I could ask. It seemed too good to be true, that he'd wash the dishes and I'd get to put on pajamas and lie down. The thought filled me with profound relief.

"Really," he said, kissing the side of my head. "And do I get points for this?" he asked, arching one eyebrow and giving me the slight, wicked smile that I loved.

"Ever so many points."

As I brushed my teeth over our postage-stamp-sized bathroom sink, I couldn't help but give a foamy-mouthed grin in the mirror. *I am the luckiest girl in the world.*

In the living room, I heard our song come on. When I walked over, Jonathan held out his hand to me and asked, "Shall we dance?"

The room was warm and dark and quiet save for Willie Nelson's voice singing "Moonlight in Vermont." Jonathan and I had never been to Vermont together, but the song wasn't really about a particular place. Rather, it was about how love changes a landscape, how it imbues everything with beauty and meaning. We didn't have a good explanation for why it was our song. It just felt right to us, and once again, that was enough.

That afternoon, we had a small, beautiful ceremony and reception at a historic home downtown. My closest friends helped me get ready, squeezing my hands and applying my makeup. Mom pressed the wrinkles out of my satin waterfall of a dress, Dad walked me down the (very short) aisle, and Willie remained blessedly, remarkably calm throughout the ceremony.

Afterward, Jonathan and I stood outside on the mansion's wide front porch, stunned as hatchlings in the sun. It was like seeing the light at the end of a long, dark tunnel.

THAT BRINGS US TO the interesting thing about the "Monte Cristo" approach: while the fictional Dantes spent years digging the tunnel, he actually escaped from prison by wrapping himself in his friend Faria's body bag and getting thrown out to sea. (Desperate times, desperate measures.)

You could say that there's no clear, direct link between the tunnel Dantes dug and the way he got out. But I would argue otherwise.

The act of digging the tunnel with Faria was critical. Without that, Dantes would not have been in any shape to discern his true way out. He would have missed the opportunity. He had to practice his defiance; the daily digging prepared him to seize his best chance for escape. The process also prepared him for the death of his old identity as a prisoner. It's no accident that Dantes left the prison in a body bag. In a symbolic sense, he had to die to get out.

What about you? What do you want to create in your life? What prison do you want to escape, and what freedom calls out to you? What old identity are you willing to let die so that you can really live? And are you ready to start digging?

Yes, digging your tunnel might take longer than you think it should. Scratch that—it almost certainly will. But the digging itself will change you. Little by little, it will make you stronger.

Recovering perfectionists like us think we need to find the single grand gesture that will break our old bonds once and for all. But what we really need is the willingness to practice taking humble, quietly defiant actions on a regular basis.

This looks like saying yes when we mean yes and no when we mean no. It means sharing our personal decisions without overexplaining or justifying them to others. It involves paying close attention to our words and speaking more directly: "I've decided to do this." "I've decided to pass on that."

It entails enduring uncomfortable silences and sometimes hanging up the phone. It's about acknowledging that we cannot please everyone all of the time and that it is not our job to micromanage other people's emotional lives. (They are allowed to feel angry or disappointed, after all.) It means reminding ourselves, "I do not owe anyone an explanation. But I do owe myself a revolution."

THE NO-OWE INVITATION

Change Your Language, Change Your Life

The words we choose play a big part in our transformation; they can help us feel free or keep us feeling trapped.

For the next week, practice changing the way you speak about yourself and your life. Our words both reflect and shape our experience, and it's possible to impact your felt experience by changing your language.

To cite just one study in which researchers looked at the speech patterns of people with depression, "If [depressive] symptoms are indeed partially organized by language structure, a treatment approach to normalizing of language might play a beneficial role in improving affective state."

This is scientific-speak for, "If you use more empowered language, you just might feel better!"

With that in mind, notice the times and places where you are explaining yourself. Pay closer attention. Whenever you hear it happen, pause. Catch yourself. When you are aware that you are justifying yourself, interrupt the pattern and say something different!

Personally, I've noticed that I tend to overexplain my decisions when I'm feeling tired or anxious. If I hear myself do it, I make a point to change course, playfully.

For example, I might say, "I decided to go to the library first even though I didn't get to all of my emails because I knew I had client calls later . . . oops, I'm overexplaining! I do not have do to that anymore. I'm free to do what I want, no explanation needed. So, backspace! Control, alt, delete!"

When I feel stuck in apology energy, I also quote this line from *Jane Eyre*: "I am no bird; and no net ensnares me; I am a free human being with an independent will." I actually feel my spine straighten when I say it.

You can also enlist supportive loved ones to help you become aware of your overexplanations. That said, make sure you select someone who can prompt you in a helpful, respectful way. Jonathan knows that I appreciate it when he says, quietly, "You're explaining again." This is a good prompt for me, and it registers as loving, not shaming.

For a bonus challenge, remove words and phrases such as *can't*, *have to*, *should*, and *must* from your vocabulary, unless they are literally true. "I can't push this ten-ton boulder uphill alone" is literally true; "I can't call my grandmother on her birthday" may not be.

Replace your usual words and phrases with more accurate ones, such as *I don't want to*, *I'm already booked*, *It's not a priority for me*, and *I'm choosing something else right now*.

For example, instead of saying, "I can't go to the party," you might say, "Thank you so much for inviting me! I'm not available at that time; I already have another commitment." And instead of saying, "Oh, I'm so tired, but I have to go take care of the baby," you might say, "I'm choosing to go take care of the baby, even though right now I feel tired."

This exercise helps you feel more in command of your own life. Try it and see what shifts! (I've used this practice for years, and though it's popular with many coaches, I first heard about it from Martha Beck and Katherine North.)

9

You Don't Owe Anyone
Your Time and Energy

Leaving because you want to doesn't mean you pack your
bags the moment there's strife or struggle or uncertainty.
It means that if you yearn to be free of a particular
relationship and you feel that yearning lodged within you
more firmly than any of the other competing and contrary
yearnings are lodged, your desire to leave is not only valid,
but probably the right thing to do. Even if someone you love
is hurt by that.

—Cheryl Strayed, *Tiny Beautiful Things*

IT USED TO BE good, right? That job, that relationship, that volunteer position—whatever it was, it started out fine. But over time,
things changed. Or maybe you did. Either way, you're walking around
with a secret truth: you want to leave.

You don't want to admit this to anyone. You're steadfast, you're
patient, and you do not bail at the first sign of trouble. You stand by
your people. These are beautiful qualities. But sometimes, old loy-
alties blind you. Instead of seeing that things need to change, you

rationalize, "It's not really that bad." Yet you're increasingly uncomfortable, exhausted, or likely both. It's not a good setup for you any longer.

So when is it wise to say, "Enough"?

When your deepest truth is that you want to.

Maybe this sounds simple. And in some ways it is, but it's also quite difficult to put into practice because it means dealing with the multitude of voices in your head.

First, there's the voice of shame saying, "Who do you think you are to consider leaving? You're a terrible, selfish person for even thinking about it!" If you want to leave a job, then there's also the fearful voice of scarcity saying, "Don't you dare quit, or you'll end up a bag lady!" Finally, there's the fearsome, emotional debt-collector harpy calling, "These people and this organization have been good to you! And this is such a good cause! You owe it your time and energy! You can't just leave!"

When I was in my early twenties, I let those voices sway me. As a result, I jammed myself into jobs that fit neither the woman I was nor the woman I was becoming.

———

MY BACKPACK BANGED AGAINST my spine as I sprinted toward the bus stop. *Please, please, let me catch a 43 bus today*, I prayed. As I pushed my leaden legs faster, I thought back over my Tuesday morning routine. How very hard it had been to leave the nest of our bed, with its cozy comforter! When I'd first started work as a L'Arche Arlington program director, I'd had no problem rising on time, walking the half mile to the bus stop on Columbia Road, and boarding an 8:00 a.m. bus. Nearly two years later, I struggled to catch the same bus even though Jonathan and I had moved to an apartment just around the corner from the stop. (The apartment brought to mind the classic Mastercard commercial framework—rent for a tiny studio in the Adams Morgan neighborhood: $1,100/month. Cost of student loans:

$300/month. The ability to make coffee and eat breakfast without talking to anyone: *priceless*.)

Even so, the studio space was not ideal for two people working very different hours and desperate for sleep. Jonathan had moved into a leadership role on the L'Arche house team, which meant that he did all of his usual caregiving routines plus additional administrative work. He was just as tired as I was.

Though I'd planned to respond to new work emails before setting out, I'd had just enough time to click through a half dozen of them before slamming down the lid of my laptop and shoving it between full-to-bursting file folders in my backpack.

Rounding the corner in a sprint, I heard the telltale screech of bus brakes. The yellow-lit numbers atop the bus read 43. *Hallelujah.* A 43 bus would skip several stops and avoid the insanity that was Dupont Circle at rush hour. Moreover, the bus wasn't packed full yet. I glimpsed a few empty seats.

Thank you, God! I thought as I scanned my WMATA SmarTrip card and sank into the first available seat. *A 43 and a place to sit.*

Shifting in my seat, I took a deep breath and reached for my water bottle. I'd run just one block, but already perspiration gathered under my arms. Reaching forward, I double-checked my backpack for deodorant and a backup shirt. The distance between our apartment and L'Arche Arlington totaled just 7.9 miles, but without a car, my public-transit commute took at least seventy-five minutes each way.

Though Jonathan had a very short commute, his workdays came with their own set of difficulties, including an inflexible schedule. When we said goodnight each Monday evening, we did so knowing that we wouldn't cross paths conscious until Wednesday night at the earliest. All L'Arche assistants were assigned tasks outside of their caregiving routines, and Jonathan's skills kept netting him additional responsibilities. As if all of that wasn't enough, both of us carried emergency on-call phones on a rotating basis.

I pulled my backpack into my lap. *I really should review my outline for the meeting with the case manager later today*, I thought, but I didn't draw out my steno notebook. I just stared out the window, noticing the disappointed looks on the faces of other commuters gathered at subsequent stops.

I'd made the bus—and the life—that everyone else seemed to want. I had a stable, meaningful job with health-care benefits. I had the flexibility to work from home once a week. I had a husband I loved and a caring community that valued and supported us both. I was fortunate, and I knew it.

But still, tears prickled behind my eyes. I averted my face so my seatmate wouldn't see the surge of emotion. *What is going on here?* I wondered. *What am I even feeling? Sad* was the obvious choice, but as I leaned my head against the bus windowpane, a more truthful answer arose: *Angry. I am really, really pissed off.*

Mentally I walked back through my morning routine, trying to pinpoint the shift from fatigue to fury. After a beat, I had it: I'd opened an email from my supervisor, a tersely worded note directing me to sign up for a day of professional training. When I'd scanned the event description, everything inside of me rebelled. The training required a four-hour round-trip drive to Richmond, Virginia. The event focused on compliance with the new Virginia Medicaid regulations, the part of my role I liked the least. It required obsessive documentation, endless filing, and increasingly restrictive rules. Frankly, the thought of going to that training made me want to throw myself under the 43 bus.

In a flash, I understood the nature of the problem. If I went to the training, I really would be throwing myself under the bus—my true self, at least. For months, I'd pushed her aside, ignoring the part of me that wanted a different life. But I was running out of energy to suppress her truth.

I'd been telling myself that I needed to do this job because it served the people I loved. I thought that I just needed to be better and stronger for them, that I just needed to give more of my time and energy to them. But after nearly two years, the role was wrecking me. It was time for me to question my thinking and the reasons why I'd taken it on in the first place.

"Any kind of job with a nurturing element to it needs to be interrogated," wrote Heather Havrilesky, "because we women view ourselves not just as failures but as terrible selfish pieces of shit when we can't give and give to infinity and beyond. . . . People with dysfunctional backgrounds who are attracted to helping professions are particularly vulnerable to this identity trap. The truth is that you can be amazingly good at helping others and still be torn to shreds by too much of it."

That was my condition. I was simultaneously very good at my job and shredded by its requirements. During one of my birthday celebrations at L'Arche, community members were asked to describe my gifts. An observant intern had written, "Caroline always finishes the job!" Alongside those words, he'd used Crayons to draw a stick-figure picture of me pulling a tray out of the house oven and flashing a competent, in-control smile. That intern had me pegged; for better or worse, I did always finish the job. But did I choose my jobs wisely? I wondered. Did I spend my time doing what I loved?

The questions had haunted me ever since my grandfather and a dear friend from L'Arche had died. As I mourned them, I understood that there was no running away from my truth any longer.

Over my harried breakfast that morning, a quick scroll through my Twitter feed turned up a Tweet from a writer and entrepreneur I admired, Ash Ambirge: "What do you want to do? That's the only question you need to answer."

I knew what I wanted to do; I had known since I was six years old. I wanted to be a writer. I wanted to make books. Even with my high-demand job, I still wrote in my journal in the mornings and on my laptop in the evenings. With Jonathan's support, I'd begun a blog highlighting lessons I'd learned from my friends with special needs at L'Arche. I'd named the site *A Wish Come Clear* in Willie's honor, a nod to the "purposeful mistakes" that he and I both loved. My prayer for the blog was that it would be like the intentional gaps in those Native American blankets that I read about on the morning that so much changed for me. I prayed that the blog would provide an opening for Spirit to move. I dreamed about building up the blog's readership and becoming a published author.

That was the life I longed for. If my time and energy actually belonged to me, I thought, that was what I wanted to do with them. So on that ordinary Tuesday morning, I wiped away my tears, disembarked the bus, and decided to do something about it.

———

FAIR WARNING: SOMETIMES, THE CHOICE to take back your time and energy actually makes your life more difficult. Once I made the decision to change careers, I worked hard to launch my freelance copywriting business in the months before I gave my notice at L'Arche. But the hard work paid off. Just three months since my last day at L'Arche, I was earning more as a freelance writer than I had as a program director. I wrote weekly columns and feature articles for an online magazine about adult autism issues, and I picked up other writing assignments whenever I could.

Now, I typed the last words of my latest column and drained the last drop of my Starbucks coffee. *OK*, I thought, *now the column is done, so that's money in the bank. And since I interviewed that expert yesterday, I can edit the feature article today.* Shifting out of the wooden café chair I'd occupied for the past two hours, I slipped on my coat and braced myself to go back out into the cold.

At first, I'd been so thrilled by self-employment that I hadn't minded working long hours alone in our tiny, dark apartment until Jonathan returned from exhausting twelve-hour days at L'Arche. When the solitude got to me, I'd treat myself to typing away at a table at Starbucks. As a fledgling entrepreneur, though, even a tall coffee at $2.25 felt like an extravagance. But I'd worked out a system to make it worthwhile. Since Starbucks offered refills, I'd work for a few hours at the Connecticut Avenue Starbucks, then take my empty coffee cup for a walk to one of the Dupont Circle stores for a $0.55 refill and a couple more hours' work outside the apartment.

But on this day, as I considered leaving one Starbucks for another, I wondered if I'd follow through on the refill plan after all. I was tired all the time, and I wasn't sleeping well. And although I didn't have a shingles rash, I felt the frightening fatigue I associated with the illness. I'd hoped that my health would get better once I left the program director role, but here I was, still feeling sick. The last doctor I'd seen had told me I was the picture of health. She'd praised me for taking excellent care of my body. But I'd left her office thinking, *If I'm the picture of health, then why do I spend most of my weekends in bed? What the hell is wrong with me?*

The problem was, I didn't fully appreciate the body's wonderful (and terrible) capacity to rebel against situations that stifle the soul. I'd pushed my body too hard for too long, and it was effectively shutting down in protest. Though I'd created a new job for myself, I was still struggling with longstanding patterns of overwork and over-responsibility. As demanding as my caregiving roles had been, there was a part of me that was more demanding still.

For perfectionists and people-pleasers like us, it's par for the course to do well in our roles. We have a tendency to keep taking on additional tasks and saying yes to new requests. We are driven and dedicated. But in order to succeed, we overgive to others. We act like we owe them our time and every ounce of our energy. In an attempt to please them, we push aside the responsibility of taking care of ourselves. And when we make that trade-off too many times, our lives start falling apart. We burn out and break down.

Yet those crashes give us an invaluable gift: the chance to see the truth about our lives. They point us in a new direction; they help us let go of the excess baggage and focus on the essential instead. The experience may feel harsh, but it's actually benevolent. Sometimes life has to get difficult in order to wake us up.

That winter day on the way home from Starbucks, I was finally sick and tired enough to listen to a whisper of possibility. Swiping my key card at our apartment building's back door with gusts of chill winter wind at my back, I daydreamed about living somewhere with a milder climate. Before he'd moved back to DC the second time, Jonathan had purchased a 1901 fixer-upper home in northwestern Alabama that he rented out, returning biannually for upkeep and maintenance. The year before, I'd come along for the ride and fallen in love with the small town. A simple knowing had arisen within me: *This could be our home. We could live here and be happy.*

Recalling that moment, I thought about how moving to Alabama would make many of our other dreams possible. Jonathan and I could slow our frantic pace and recover from caregiving burnout. Both of us wanted to work for ourselves, save money, and have a cat. (OK, *I* wanted a cat.) For so long, I had resisted the idea of leaving DC, where we had friends and community. But we wanted different jobs and a different life, and Alabama gave us a real chance at both.

Have you ever had a moment like that when you realized, *Wait a minute, if I do this one thing, it will bring all of these other dreams within reach?* Can you think of a time when you fought change with all your might, and then discovered that it was actually the best thing that could have happened? Do you remember the feeling you had when you realized that the very thing you were clinging to was the same thing holding you back?

Maybe for you, it was ending the friendship that was draining the life from your heart. Maybe it was booking the tickets and going on that trip to another country. Maybe it was wearing that red dress that you'd hidden away. Those pivot decisions are powerful, but that doesn't mean that they're easy. Reclaiming our time and energy feels subversive. It involves stepping out of our old roles and ways of being. In the process, we are bound to feel shaken and scared.

Sometimes we actually feel the most fear when we move toward something that's deeply right for us. It's similar to the boundaries concept we talked about before; just as a certain type of false guilt can be a sign of progress, a certain type of fear can indicate that we're on the right track. But how do we tell the difference? How do we know if the fear that we're feeling is a positive indicator?

To discern, I like to use this imagery from Martha Beck's book *The Joy Diet*: "A good risk feels like taking a high dive into a sparkling clean pool; a bad risk feels like taking the same leap, but into polluted swamp water." Rather than pushing the fear away, pay attention to how it feels. Taste it as you would an ice cream flavor. Is it swirled with feelings of excitement and exhilaration? Or is it marbled with awful dread?

Feel the fear with your body rather than trying to analyze it with your mind. Pay attention to how your body feels when you consider spending your precious time and energy in a certain way. Remember the "You're Getting Warmer, You're Getting Colder" exercise we did earlier; this is the same basic premise. And if you get a clear answer but then your mind immediately starts up with judgments and limiting beliefs, that's a great opportunity to question your thoughts, do The Work, and offer yourself forgiveness.

If you're serious about reclaiming your time and energy, another powerful practice is to look back at your calendar and perform an analysis of the past weeks and months. Author and former Harvard professor Tal Ben-Shahar offers an effective framework, beginning with the question, "What, for you, is worth all of the gold in Fort Knox? Can you envision something in your life that would provide you with an abundance of happiness?"

Ben-Shahar recommends recording your daily activities and assigning each one a score based on the meaning and pleasure it brings to your life. He suggests both increasing the activities that give you the most happiness and integrating happiness boosters into activities that do not bring you delight.

Even in difficult circumstances, we still have the power to choose how we allocate our time and energy. We don't owe anyone these priceless commodities. The first and most important thing to do is to remember our own power to choose rather than defaulting to powerlessness.

When we remember that we don't owe anyone, we're able to avoid the pervasive trap of the victim mentality. Again, this doesn't mean that our life circumstances will magically get easier—in fact, they may get harder for a time! But psychologically, we're much better off than we were before.

For example, we may choose to stay in a difficult situation for a specified period of time, so that we have what we need to build a different future. That's what I did in the last six months I served as a program director for L'Arche. Instead of feeling trapped, I saw those final months as stepping-stones to entrepreneurship. I understood that it was a privilege to have a job while I began building my first business. There were long, hard days in those last six months, but they felt progressive rather than Sisyphean.

If you've been feeling your life energy draining away, here's my recommendation: Feel the fear, and find your Alabama anyway. Find the one thing that is going to help you get all the other things you want. Then when you find it, fight for it. Do what it takes to make it happen. Don't settle for feeling victimized by your own life.

ON MOVING DAY, I woke up and thought, *Nothing will ever be the same again.* Soon after my moment of clarity, Jonathan and I had reached a ready agreement: After a few months of transition and preparation, we would move to Alabama and run our own virtual businesses. We would set our own schedules; we would slow down and sleep late. We would move into a house in need of major renovations, yes, but we would also leave behind our steep DC rent. It was a trade-off that we were more than willing to make. Choosing to move to an area with a lower cost of living solved a lot of problems. It eased the financial pressure on my fledgling copywriting business, and it gave us both the freedom and time we needed to recuperate from the strain of the last several years.

As we packed up our DC apartment one last time, though, ordinary objects acquired sudden sentimental value. Surrounded as I was by the relics of a disappearing life, my usual impulse to declutter turned on its head. There was a strange sadness at the thought of letting go of our old, broken Swiffer. When Jonathan asked to toss it, I actually clung to it for a moment. It had been my mom's Swiffer first, and my spoken question, "How can I let go of the Swiffer?" was code for, "How can I move so far away from my family?" I took a deep breath and reminded myself that the Swiffer was not my family, then put the pieces down the trash chute.

As Jonathan and I gathered dusty papers and bills for recycling, we uncovered an outdated L'Arche emergency-line phone charger in the detritus. The first time that phone had rung in our apartment, I'd felt a rush of adrenaline: *If anything bad happens, we have to deal with it. We are the cavalry now.* But when the excitement wore off, it was replaced by a weighty stone of dread. Chucking the charger signaled the end of being constantly available.

Just before we started loading the moving van, I unearthed my stenographer's notebook. That small volume had been my program director base camp, full of scribbled-down notes and frantic to-do lists. The notebook's pages were a sickly, old-fashioned green, with two Care Bears stickers brightening up the brown cover. I'd picked up those stickers in the waiting room of a doctor's office, when I'd accompanied a core member to an annual physical. The stickers reminded me that there were moments of joy in my job, right until the end. I loved seeing excited new assistants flying solo on routines and adults with disabilities achieving their goals. At L'Arche, there was laughter and fun and celebration. There was a sense of belonging that I knew I'd always miss.

Leaving because you want to is never black and white, and it felt bittersweet to go. Yet I knew in some bone-deep way that this exodus was necessary. It was about embodying the truth that Jonathan and I didn't owe anyone our time and energy. It was about deciding to reclaim those treasures for ourselves.

YEARS AFTER JONATHAN AND I made the move, I spoke with a potential coaching client who began our discovery call with, "I don't feel adequate enough to talk to you." (How's that for an opening line?)

This woman had reasons to feel less-than, stuck, and scared. To protect her privacy, I won't share those reasons here. It suffices to say that she had a tough history. She dreamed of helping other people but struggled to help herself. When I encouraged her to get support for her journey, she made an effort and asked for financial help from her church once. But when she didn't hear back from her contact at the church, she stopped asking. I challenged her to follow up with her church contact again, knowing that it would be difficult for her. Sometimes making the choice to save our own lives is really scary.

She said, "No. I can't . . . It's too painful." She said that God would have to step in because she wasn't willing to do any more for herself. She wanted the change, but she wasn't prepared to invest any significant time and energy to make it happen. She wasn't willing to risk disappointment.

After our meeting, I sent her a note, saying,

Given your history, it makes sense you'd struggle to reach out for help and support. But here's what I'll say: You have to rest and take care of yourself, yes, but you have also got to reach.

For you, this means following up on the request that you made. You're scared that people from your church won't support you. But the more important questions are

Will YOU support you?
Will YOU ask even if you feel uncomfortable?
Will YOU ask even if you're scared to hear no?

That's how you take a stand for what matters to you.

Yes, I know it matters what they say about your request. It matters whether they extend help. But in another sense, it doesn't matter. What matters more is whether or not YOU reach.

Your church is important to you, and so is your faith. Remember how, in the New Testament accounts, Jesus is always responding to people who reach? Remember the woman who touched his cloak after she had been bleeding for years; remember the people who lowered their paralyzed friend through the roof so he could receive healing? God does help us in miraculous ways, yes . . . and we also have to reach.

I hope that's helpful; please know that it is said with love and gentleness and a desire for you to rise. I want that for you. Will you want it for yourself?

As I typed those words, it dawned on me that I'd earned the right to write them because I had asked those questions and taken those risks. Over and over, I'd chosen to reach for new life when my old life no longer fit.

A few years after Jonathan and I moved to Alabama, I decided to let go of the successful copywriting business I'd built in order to create an even more successful coaching business. Had I not done that, I wouldn't have come into contact with this woman in the first place. Our conversation only happened because I'd reached for something that seemed outside of my grasp. I'd given my time and energy to that new endeavor, with no guarantee that it would go well.

You don't owe anyone else your time and energy, it's true. But what you do with those precious resources matters. Once, you gave away your time and energy indiscriminately. Now is your chance to steward them wisely.

Consider: What do you owe *yourself?* Whatever your dream is, this life requires you to reach for it, to take action and make it real. You must be fierce on your own behalf.

THE NO-OWE INVITATION

Clarify Your Vision for the Future

In my coaching, I've adapted and amalgamated elements of spiritual psychology along with insights from my favorite coaches, such as Martha Beck, Deborah Hurwitz, and others. This exercise represents one such mix.

To begin, choose one area of your life (such as your home, relationships, work, spirituality, or financial status) that feels less than optimal. Pick an area where you'd like to see significant change. Once you've named it, write at least one paragraph, ideally more, about how you long for this area of your life to look and feel different. Write about what this area of your life would look like if you had a magic wand and you could have it any way you want it.

This exercise is more challenging than it sounds! Often it's easier to see the places we are stuck and name something that feels wrong rather than envision what would feel right.

When I do calls with potential coaching clients, I usually lead by asking them, "What do you really want?" In many cases, people answer that question by telling me what they *don't* want. "Well, I don't want to feel so tired." Gently, I redirect them: "Yes, I hear that you don't want to feel so tired. So what *do* you want? How do you want to feel?"

If they're stuck, I frame the question as an opposite: "What's the opposite of tired, for you?" Often their voices brighten as they say the words: "Energized. Enthusiastic. Excited." If you're struggling to describe what you want, the "opposite game" may be a helpful jump-start.

While you might wish to change everything about your life at once, begin by picking one area of your life and writing about what would be ideal for you. (Choosing one area to start helps prevent overwhelm.) To take the example of improving your sleep and increasing your energy, what does that look like, ideally?

As you write, ground your description of external realities with internal realities. To give a simple example, it's all well and good to say that you want to trade your creaky futon for a real bed, but why? How do you imagine that making that external change will affect your internal feeling state?

Instead of simply writing, "I want to sleep in a real bed, not on a lumpy futon!" expand on the motivation behind the desire: "I want to feel energized, abundant, and richly rested when I wake up in my full-size bed."

Once you've written at least a paragraph, take five to seven statements and shape them into affirmations. State your ideal reality in the present tense, using the following structure: "I am [feeling a certain way] [doing a certain thing]." Or put another way, "I am [adverb or adverbs] [verb or verb phrase] [description]."

For example,

I am peacefully sleeping in my new, comfortable bed.
I am happily and easily going to sleep each night in my new bed.
I am gratefully waking up in my new bed, feeling energized and
    ready to greet the new day.

Also note that instead of making a "freedom from negative" statement, such as "I'm free from insomnia," you state the desire in more positive terms: "I'm falling asleep easily each night." It's much easier for your mind to imagine the latter than the former.

Write down your finished statements, including "This or something better for the highest good of all concerned," at the bottom of the page. (I'm not sure who coined that statement, but I first heard it at The Clearing.) That final sentence makes room for all the wonderful possibilities you cannot imagine yet.

You can use the same process for each significant area of your life, from your family to your finances. You can also create a personal affirmation statement summing up what you seek to embody and experience throughout your life. As of this writing, my personal affirmation is: "I am a strong, courageous, beautiful woman, living in my integrity, loving myself first and then others."

A quick note on belief here—as you create your vision and affirmation statements, you will probably get some significant pushback from your own thoughts: "That's not realistic! You tried before and failed! You don't deserve that! You're not good enough to say that!" If that's what comes up for you, I understand; when I first spoke the words, "Loving myself first and then others," the people-pleasing part of me had a meltdown. A trusted counselor recommended that I integrate that phrase, and it was a real stretch for me. Much as I longed to claim self-love sovereignty, the words felt terribly taboo. (In hindsight, I was scared to make the shift from Sacrificial Giver to Otherish Giver that we talked about earlier.)

So if that's your experience, just know that you are not alone. Don't resist the resistance. Rather, simply observe your mind thinking those thoughts, knowing that it is just trying to keep you safe and stop you from changing. Instead of trying to get rid of the thoughts, write them down so that you can question them using The Work of Byron Katie or another process. Then carry on creating your vision and affirmation statements, knowing that it's perfectly normal and expected for your mind to freak out. Remember, you do not actually have to make any concrete changes right now. Just allow yourself to be honest about what you want. When you've spent years pushing down your desires, this truth-telling is a significant step.

The final step of this process is to energize your vision in a way that feels right for you. Some people post the paper in a place where they'll see it often, and some record themselves reading the affirmations aloud and play back the track daily. Whatever you choose, don't just make it rote repetition; focus on actually inhabiting your vision and feeling into the way you want to feel. This exercise is about creating a container for the feeling state that you want to experience. It's about giving yourself the gift of spending time in a reality where your dreams have already come to pass.

10

You Don't Owe Anyone

an Interaction

> My life was narrated for me by others. Their voices were
> forceful, emphatic, absolute. It had never occurred to me
> that my voice might be as strong as theirs.
>
> —Tara Westover, *Educated*

ISN'T IT INTERESTING HOW we hide the truth of what we think and feel in order to "preserve" our relationships? We tell lies about what we do and don't want, or we lie by omission to avoid conflict. We bring a false self to the table, then get upset when we don't feel a sense of intimacy with our people. Of course we don't. They don't know who we really are, and in some sense, neither do we. We've been pretending for so long that we've lost track. Operating this way is like going without food; the longer we deprive ourselves of true connection, the weaker we get.

Deep down we know this, yet we also resist the knowing. We work hard to maintain our false friendships; we spend lots of time trying to fix connections that lack a firm foundation. We hustle at something that has never worked in the past and is not working now. We think we need to do more, but what if we need to do less? What if we need to stop pretending? What if we don't owe anyone an interaction, least of all a pretend one? What would our lives look like if we believed that?

"What good is it for someone to gain the whole world, yet forfeit their soul?" Jesus once asked. But you already know the answer. You've run the experiment, haven't you? What good is it for you to gain praise, money, friendship, or familial approval if you've forfeited the truth of who you are in order to get it?

It's no good at all. It's soulless success.

But what if you start being truer to yourself, and then people reject you? What if you summon up the courage to stop pretending, and then you get slammed for it?

There are so many versions of this worry; though the wording changes, the core fear is the same: What if I do what is true for me and then bad things happen?

What if I respectfully decline to comply with an unreasonable request, and the person who asked sends me a whole series of shaming emails?

What if my essay gets published on that big news site, but then people post comments criticizing everything from my ethics to my personal appearance?

What if I tell my friend that I'm not available to do that last-minute favor she asked of me, and she decides that our long-term friendship is over?

In one sense, these are legitimate concerns. Even if we plan carefully, speak kindly, and navigate change as diplomatically as possible, those things we fear may happen. Actually, every one of those scenarios outlined previously *has* happened to me. To put it mildly, not everyone is comfortable with hearing and telling the truth. Not everyone is ready to love the real you. Some people will, and you'll grow closer than ever. It will be wonderful! And some people will freak out. They will fly into a rage or shame you into silence if you dare to give voice to what is true for you.

That is a hard reality. It's rough when people you love think you are wrong or bad or crazy. Losing their approval will hurt, at least for a little while. But what actually hurts more (and has already been hurting you more) is you rejecting yourself. You're scared that they'll reject you, but you've already rejected you.

What if you decided to stop doing that? After all, it hasn't nourished your soul. Maybe now you are hungry enough, tired enough, and thirsty enough to try another way.

How would your life look different if you didn't owe anyone an interaction?

If that idea shocks you, consider this: Interacting over and over again when we really don't want to actually erodes our ability to be kind. It leads to resentment and anger. But when we let go of the expectation, that takes the pressure off. Instead of feeling burdened with "shoulds," we feel free and expansive; we're connected to an authentic generosity.

When you don't owe anyone an interaction, you're free to give from the heart.

You're also free to assume authority over your own life. In one of my favorite podcast episodes, author and speaker Rob Bell recounts a scene from the film *Chariots of Fire*. He quotes two lines of dialogue regarding an unexpectedly proposed switch to the Olympic roster:

"That's a matter for the committee!" one older man says, with consternation in his voice.

Immediately, the man next to him says, "We *are* the committee."

In other words: we are the decision-makers. The authority to decide this matter is not located elsewhere; it's right here with us, as close as our own hearts. We are the ones who make the choices. In that spirit, Rob Bell asks a provocative question: "How many times have you been searching for that which you already possess?"

We search outside ourselves for guidance, validation, and permission. But we already have everything we need. We *are* the committee already.

Nevertheless, it can be difficult to remember that when you're spending time with the people who have been your primary authority figures for most of your life.

BEEP. BEEP. BEEP. The alarm clock I'd set at the Pittsburgh hotel the night before blared, jolting me from deep sleep. I shuddered, burrowing more deeply into my nest of fluffy blankets. *Five more minutes,* I thought, reaching my bare arm into the air-conditioned chill just long enough to smack the insistent beeping into silence. *Just a little more time. Then I'll get up and get ready to drive with my mom to the convention center. Oh my God, I get to speak today!*

Then I heard my mother's voice, half shouting over the buzz of the air conditioner: "'The heavens declare the glory of God; the skies proclaim the work of his hands!'"

"What the . . . ?" I mumbled, not loud enough for Mom to hear. My head was still under the covers; it seemed safer there. My arms and legs were frozen in place. *How does one respond to a top-volume recitation of Psalm 19 before breakfast?*

"'Day after day they pour forth speech; night after night they reveal knowledge!'"

Surrendering to the sunshine that flooded our hotel room, I stretched and pushed myself up to a sitting position. "What are you *doing?*"

My voice came out pleading, almost desperate. The day before, Mom and I had taken turns driving the family minivan six hours from northern New Jersey to Pittsburgh, Pennsylvania. The day before that, I'd taken a car ride and two flights north from Alabama. (Jonathan and I had been married for four years, but each year I traveled to New Jersey to visit friends and family while he held down the fort at home.) And today I'd lead a breakout session titled, "The Challenges and Joys of Being a Sibling" at the forty-fourth annual Autism Society of America convention. It was 2013, and this was my biggest speaking engagement to date.

"Good morning, Cari!" Mom chimed, bounding over to my bed with her gilt-edged Bible in hand. "It's a beautiful day to praise God with a psalm. He is amazing! Listen to this." She flipped forward a few pages, getting ready to read again.

"Mom, I. Just. Woke. Up. Seriously! There has been no *coffee*."

"Oh," Mom said. "OK." Turning away, she closed her Bible, her enthusiasm dimmed.

I swallowed hard and chose my next words with care. "Mom, I really appreciate you coming with me on this trip. I do. It's just that I'm not even fully conscious and you're . . . um . . . proclaiming Bible verses at me."

It feels manipulative, I thought but didn't say. Intuitively, I sensed that Mom's recitation was related to the conversation we'd had in the car the day before. On the drive to Pittsburgh, Mom had asked me if I read my Bible, and for the first time, I'd risked telling her my truth: "When you ask me that question, I feel uncomfortable because I'm thinking that you're trying to score me spiritually. It sounds like you're feeling concerned, needing reassurance that I prioritize quiet time with God. I do."

From there, I had opened up about my current spiritual practices. I'd told my mom about how I meditated and read good books and walked into cold creeks on hot days. She hadn't said much, though I got the sense that my outside-of-the-box answer was unsettling for her.

"OK, I get it," Mom said. "No more Bible verses before coffee."

I sighed with relief. "Just let me get dressed, and then we can hit the breakfast bar."

At the convention center, Mom smiled and shook hands and was a model of motherly support. My talk went well, and afterward she hugged me and told me that she was proud. I was elated, but cautiously so. Mom meant her kind words of affirmation, I knew. But I also sensed that it would be hard for her to stay with those good feelings of happiness and pride.

I'd begun to recognize that—to use the term from author Gay Hendricks—all of us have "upper limits" of how much happiness and joy we'll allow ourselves to receive. I noticed that after close, connected moments, Mom would counterbalance with conflict. I noticed this pattern because I did the same thing, except that my conflict was more internalized and hers was more externalized. When happiness felt like too much for me, I'd tamper down on the good feelings with self-judgment.

As I drove the minivan out of Pittsburgh, sheets of rain poured down and rendered the road a blur of brake lights. My shoulders tensed; I didn't like driving in the rain. *This is going to be one tough road trip*, I thought. As if on cue, Mom began speaking about the sinfulness of homosexuality.

"I mean, it's just so wrong," she said with a grimace. "On TV, they make it out to be this fun, modern thing, but really! It's a perversion of God's plan."

I kept my eyes on the road and my mouth shut, hoping she'd take the hint and change the topic. She didn't.

"And all of this fuss about gay marriage—it's ridiculous. Marriage is between a man and a woman, don't you think?" She paused, tilting her head so that she could look directly at me.

I'd spent years discreetly switching off Focus on the Family radio broadcasts at my parents' house in hopes of avoiding this very conversation. I knew what Mom expected me to say, and I remembered how I'd been taught to think when I lived at home. But going away to college had changed my perspective. I'd become friends with more people in the LGBTQ community, and I simply couldn't believe that it was wrong for them to be who they were and love who they loved.

Still, I didn't feel ready to share that perspective with my mom, not behind the wheel in a rainstorm on an unfamiliar highway. My shoulders twitched, and the skin under my arms prickled. "Mom, could we please not talk about this right now, when I'm driving in the rain?"

She wasn't having it. "Do you think that homosexuality is a sin?"

Well, here we are, I thought, gripping the steering wheel with sweaty palms. I could have declined to participate in the conversation; I recognized that as an option. I didn't owe her this interaction. But did I owe it to myself? I couldn't help but think of my friends at Vassar; I saw their faces in my mind's eye. I could almost feel them in the car with me, waiting to see whether I would pass judgment. It seemed important that I tell my truth.

"Actually, no," I replied, quietly. "I don't."

"What do you *mean*, you don't?" Mom cried out. "*Caroline!* I can't believe you! The Bible tells us that it's a sin!"

Thunder boomed overhead, and the bottom of my stomach fell out. A bolt of lightning shot across the sky, a brilliant arc of electricity that lit up the highway. The windshield wipers kept up their steady swish, but the rhythm of my breath sped up. I was surrounded by my mother's disapproval, the very thing I'd always feared. With a sidelong glance, I saw that she was flushed with frustration, and also . . . was it fear?

After I took a deep breath, I said, "I hear you, and I know that some Bible verses have been interpreted that way. But there are other ways to read them."

Knowing that an argument outside of the biblical context wouldn't carry weight with my mom, I spoke about Scripture. I shared what I'd learned from speakers and writers such as Glennon Doyle and Matthew Vines. I outlined the reasons why I believed that being gay and being a person of faith were not mutually exclusive. All the while sweat poured out of me, soaking through my jacket and then my shirt. Mom interjected and raised her voice several times, but she listened, and I did my best to listen too.

About twenty minutes into our conversation, the rain faded into a gentle drizzle. I clicked the windshield wipers into a lower gear and thought about the last thing I wanted to say.

"Here's what I think," I said. "I think it's best to err on the side of grace. You know? I mean, maybe you and I don't agree about whether or not homosexuality is sinful, but I think we can agree that there's room for doubt. There's room for debate about what those ancient scriptures really mean for us here, now, today. Love is the greatest commandment, right? So if there is any doubt, I choose to err on the side of love. For me, that means choosing to support my friends who are gay and want to be married someday. If I turn out to be wrong about that in some cosmic sense, that's a mistake I'll be *proud* to have made because I'll have made it out of love. I think that a loving God would understand that. I have to believe that God is infinitely more understanding and more compassionate than I am."

There was a little pocket of silence in the car, a brief moment when neither of us said anything. I heard a faint rumble of thunder in the distance. I thought about the God of my childhood, the one who brought down wrath and destruction on anyone who dared to disobey. And I thought about the Presence I'd come to trust, the one who stayed close and didn't judge.

Then Mom said softly, "I do understand what you're saying. And I love you, honey."

"I love you too," I said. It was a half-strangled statement—a croak from a dry, tightened throat—but it was still true. Reaching out for the center console, I took a swig of water from my bottle. With levity in my voice, I asked, "And now, please, for the love of all that is good and holy, can we change the subject? I just gave a huge presentation, and I'm driving through a thunderstorm, and my mom wants to debate hot-button theological issues with me! I mean, I am soaked in sweat here! Are you seeing this?"

I raised my arms so that Mom could see the swooping, damp arcs on my blazer.

And then somehow we were both laughing, and the gray sky looked less heavy as we hurtled down the highway toward home.

THAT CONVERSATION HAPPENED BECAUSE in Alabama, I had that most dangerous of all combinations: time and space to think. Since my life had grown quieter, long-buried truths had come to my attention. One of those truths was the feeling of intense grief and anger that arose whenever I tried to read my Bible and attend church. I visited several congregations in hopes of finding a church home in our new hometown, but mostly I felt that old, sickening sense of cage bars coming down.

Those emotional responses led me to Google *The Worldwide Church of God* for the first time. I devoured the search results in great gulps, learning a whole new vocabulary of terms including *spiritual abuse* and *thought reform* and *cult*. As I read, I learned that what defines a cult isn't unorthodox beliefs but rather manipulative behaviors and shame-based environments characterized by control.

In the WCG, there had been no room for dissent. Once as a child, I'd witnessed a male visitor question our WCG pastor about the Saturday Sabbath doctrine during a sermon. As the words came out of the visitor's mouth, I felt the collective intake of breath in the congregation, the breach of the unspoken taboo. Just as I knew he would, the pastor politely but firmly shut down the question without answering it. No one needed to tell me that the questioner wouldn't be coming back to our church.

I learned to keep my questions to myself at church and to hide my truths from people outside the church as well. I became a spin doctor, highlighting the positives and omitting the troubling details. When people asked me about the WCG, I'd say, "Well, it was a quirky church with a lot of weird rules ... but I made some great friends! And I went to summer camp in Scotland!" I told this partial truth so often that I believed it to be whole.

During my first summer in Alabama, though, I had a dream in which I walked into an unfamiliar, single-story house in search of luggage I'd stored there. I needed to retrieve my bags, but the objects in the house kept shifting. One minute something was *here*, the next, *there*. It was as though the house itself was gaslighting me, setting me up to question my senses and feel crazy. I wondered, *Am I just being paranoid?* Yet the empty, ordinary-looking house triggered deep fear in me. I sprinted out the front door, leaving most of my bags behind.

That nightmare woke me up, both literally and metaphorically. I began to read books and articles about the psychology of control and cultic relationships. I watched the independent film *Paradise Recovered* with tears pouring down my cheeks, grateful to writer and producer Andie Redwine for taking the raw material of her own experience in the WCG and molding it into a beautiful, redemptive story. I had epic conversations with Tam about the unhealthy beliefs and practices within our childhood church; I had epic conversations with Brooke about the abuses I'd been blind to before.

When I initiated discussions about the WCG with other friends, however, I began to understand that not all church families were alike.

Mandy told me that she'd once asked her mother, "Do you remember all of the crazy stuff that the church used to teach?"

Her mother had said, "Oh yes, I remember. But I didn't believe all that, not really. I just wanted to be with my friends!"

How dissimilar our experiences had been! Whereas Eva and Mandy's moms were relatively relaxed about the WCG's rules and doctrines, mine and Tam's were stricter, more sold-out for the system.

As I compared notes with friends, I also started meeting with a professional counselor. At first, the choice to seek counseling felt taboo. As far as I knew, no one in my immediate family had been to counseling. It just wasn't done. But when I hesitated, I remembered the voice of my inner wisdom after I'd woken up shaking from my nightmare: *Yes, honey, go back into the house, and take people you trust with you. Go for those things you left behind, those things that were stolen from you when you were just a child. Go back and take what's yours by right.*

⟋

IN THE HAPPILY-EVER-AFTER VERSION of life, Mom and I would have had a new and improved relationship born like a baptism out of that rainy car conversation. I would have set stronger boundaries for myself, and Mom would have let up on the religious pressure. But life is not a Disney movie. Less than a week after the Pittsburgh trip, Mom asked me to go to church with her, and I said no. She protested, but for once I didn't waver. This refusal led to more conflict, not less. When we discussed the reasons I didn't want to go back to the WCG, it was as though we were speaking different languages.

When she read the essays I wrote about my experience in the church, she let me know that she was upset. She cited my old school paper as evidence of my unreliable memory: "Oh, you're always making up stories and making things sound worse than they were. Remember when you wrote that we waited three days to take you to the doctor after you broke your arm? That wasn't true!" This incident had been her trump card for a long time, and I used to back down whenever she brought it up. This time, though, I kept writing and publishing pieces anyway. I began to believe that I had a right to tell my own story rather than keeping it secret.

Yet since a part of me still believed that if I just found the right words, I could resolve our conflict, I called my mom over Christmas at my in-laws' and risked speaking about my church experience once more.

"Mom, it's like this. Just because we love and cherish Willie doesn't mean that life with him isn't ever difficult! Sometimes he hurts himself, and sometimes he hurts us. And sometimes he's the smartest and funniest guy. Willie isn't all good or all bad, and neither was the WCG."

I paced around my in-laws' driveway as I spoke, trying to stay calm and grounded. "It's not either/or; it's both/and," I concluded. "In order for me to feel sane, I need to be honest about the whole story. I need to talk and write about what our family and our church was really like for me, personally. I know that church was different for you as an adult. You have your own experience, and I respect that. I'm just writing about what it was like for me to be a part of the church as a kid."

"Well," Mom huffed, "your father said it best when I showed him your blog: 'That church gave her far more than it ever took.' And that's what I think too."

I tried to do the mental math. Did that statement ring true for me? Did the WCG's legalism and coercion weigh less than the friendships? Did the real relationships count for more than the extortion and lies?

"In the end, yes. The good did outweigh the bad," I said, slowly. Yet the words sounded hollow and oversimplified even as I said them.

"So there you go," Mom said, satisfied. "See? God always knows what he's doing."

Mom changed the subject, but I couldn't follow the thread of our conversation any longer. When we hung up, I was left with an acute, aching sadness. I looked up through the leaves of the trees, a sudden shaft of afternoon sun stinging my face along with Dad's quoted words and Mom's spoken ones.

Those words hurt because they minimized, because they swept away what I'd lost.

Maybe my parents couldn't look back with me at the WCG and see what I saw. Maybe they wouldn't ever call it a cult. But maybe I could stop expecting them to. Maybe I could choose to look back on the many times when they did show up for me. I could remember their generosity, all of the books and birthday cards and ballet lessons, and the massive amounts of time and energy that parents give and children take for granted. I could choose to believe that they did the best they could.

WE'VE ALL HAD CONVERSATIONS where no matter how hard we tried, we just couldn't connect on a deeper level. We've spoken our most truthful words—the ones that took all sorts of bravery for us to get out—yet our message wasn't heard. When we share our stories, we want so much for our loved ones to understand, to hear us and see us—but what if they cannot?

It hurts. When people we love aren't willing or able to go where we're going, it stings. And there's a very specific sting that comes when we get healthier emotionally and our loved ones don't register the change as positive.

If that's your experience, here are some key points to remember. First, humans don't have the greatest track record of dealing with change. Even though on some level we recognize that life is always in flux, change tends to bring up Big Feelings for us. Unexpected change in particular presses on all of our psychological pain points. The point is that even a very positive change on your part still represents a change for those you love. On one hand, they may be really happy for you, and on the other hand, they may be freaked out.

In my experience, it helps to depersonalize their response. Consider: What if their fear isn't about me and my unique changes at all? What if it's just as simple as the fear that if I change, they'll lose me?

If you think that's the case for your loved ones, try acknowledging the change and offering them reassurance. Tell them about how you're doing, and share how much they matter to you. For example, you might say something like, "Yes, this is a big change, and right now I'm feeling really good about it. I love you, and our relationship is important to me. I want us to be close. I can't wait to invite you to [be a part of something in my new life]."

That's just one example, and it won't work in every situation (which we'll talk more about later). But in many cases, a little reassurance goes a long way.

Recently, my close friend Tam made some long-awaited changes in her life. She created a new company and made some great new friends too. And even though I was thrilled for her, and even though we've been friends for a very long time, I still felt some fear and anxiety along the way. At one point, I was scared that I wouldn't be able to "keep up" with her new, evolving self. I imagined that she wouldn't want to be my friend anymore.

Fortunately, I was able to notice that these were my insecurities, not Tam's problems. I was able to take a look at myself rather than launching what Martha Beck calls a "change-back attack" and subtly or not-so-subtly trying to get Tam to go back to the way she used to be. After I spent time with these feelings on my own and did some of the healing work I've outlined in this book, I decided to be vulnerable and share my experience with Tam on a phone call.

I said something like, "I love you so much, and I'm so proud of you for making these changes. And, because I trust you, I want to share that I've been feeling a little scared. I want you to know that when I was quiet on the phone a week ago, I was wrestling with my own fear. I share that because I want you to know that I wasn't sitting in judgment of your choices. Rather, I was feeling scared that maybe there wouldn't be space for our friendship in your new life.

"And I wanted to tell you the truth about that fear, even though I feel really silly and small right now! I know that the fear goes way back for me, and it's not your job to fix or heal any of that. That's my work, and I'm doing it. But in the meantime, would you be willing to share with me how you're actually feeling about our friendship, so I'm not making myself crazy in my own head imagining how you might feel?"

Immediately, Tam offered reassurance and shared how she felt about our friendship. When we hung up, I felt closer rather than farther apart. Today, our bond is stronger than ever.

Whether you share your experience with your loved one depends on the type of relationship you have with them. But whether you choose to voice your experience or not, have compassion for your scared self. Go gently and be kind. Rather than judging yourself as "bad," offer comfort and reassurance. Pretend that you are your own parent and say to yourself what you wish your parent would say to you. For example, "Oh, honey! Of course you're scared. You love this person so much, and they're changing! Of course you feel some big feelings about that. It's all right. You can have your big feelings, and I'll be here for you through all of it. I love you."

This is a powerful realization: when we are loving toward ourselves, we also become safe harbors for others. Other people can sense whether we are kind to ourselves or whether we beat ourselves down with judgment. Tam summed it up for me this way: "The more insecure the other person is, the less safe I feel when I'm with them."

That brings us to another important point: your loved one's response to your decisions may have very little to do with what's happening right now and a whole lot to do with what happened when they were younger. For many of us, the fear of being left out and left behind goes back to kindergarten!

One of my favorite teachers, Joe Koelzer of The Clearing, talks about how when you notice someone acting like a five-year-old, chances are, *that's exactly what's happening*. Something in the present has triggered their unhealed emotional wounds, and now they're regressing, fussing, or throwing a tantrum. They're reverting back to a little-kid state, to whatever age they were when they experienced their unresolved trauma.

Of course, this doesn't excuse bad behavior, and it certainly doesn't absolve our fellow adults of responsibility for their actions. But it is helpful to understand the mechanism behind certain emotional meltdowns; it helps us have compassion for other people when they seem to be acting crazy.

All of that said, there will be times when we do our best to tell our truths and offer reassurance, and the other person still won't respond well. They may launch a full-on "change-back attack," complete with words of judgment, shame, and blame. They may even resort to physical or emotional violence.

This is a very hard truth: Some people do not have our best interests at heart. And no matter how much we love them, they may not be willing or able to treat us with respect. Will we ever fully understand their reasons for acting this way? Maybe not. Regardless, we need to look at what we *do* know and understand, which is that the relationship as it exists now is not safe for us. We can believe in the other person's potential to evolve and heal, and we can also take ourselves out of the picture while that evolution and healing is happening. We can wish another person well and also choose not spend time in their presence.

We don't owe them an interaction, and they don't owe us one either. It goes both ways. We are free, and they are free. The question is, What will we choose to do with our freedom?

For example, will we choose to stay in abusive situations when doing so is unloving to ourselves and to the other person? After all, it's not loving to allow ourselves to be abused, and it's not loving to the other person to make ourselves available for their abuse.

In *Inner Bonding*, Margaret Paul shares a great framework for setting boundaries around such behavior: "I'm not available." For example, "I'm not available to be blamed." "I'm no longer available to be criticized." "I'm not available to be yelled at." If the behavior continues after we state the boundary, we leave.

If you've been stuck in a dysfunctional pattern for a long time, the other person may not react well when you change. Ideally, they will listen and respect the boundary. But often, they will ramp up their undesired behavior in an attempt to break your boundary. They will test whether you're really serious about the new limit.

In psychological terms, this is called an "extinction burst." When the old, unhealthy norm is threatened by your new, healthier behavior, the other person puts up a big fuss and tries harder to keep the old pattern going. It's particularly important to hold your new boundaries through this kerfuffle while the dust settles and the new norm is established. (It's somewhat similar to how little kids wail and protest when their parents are getting ready to leave them with the usual babysitter. If the parents say a loving goodbye and then just keep moving out the door, about ninety seconds later, the kids have accepted the new normal and are on to the next thing.)

That said, sometimes the extinction burst isn't nearly so innocuous. If you have reason to believe that speaking your truths and setting boundaries will expose you to any physical, mental, emotional, or spiritual harm, please pause here. Trust yourself and your own inner knowing—and also, do *not* go it alone. Enlist the support of qualified helpers such as therapists, trained mental-health professionals, lawyers, or law-enforcement personnel. In serious cases of abuse, the best move may not be to speak your boundaries aloud but rather to enact them by exiting the relationship and going no-contact for your own safety.

Again, these are tough realities. But it has helped me to remember that—in the words of my college roommate, whose senior-year science project disproved her original hypothesis—"a negative result is still a result. A negative result is significant."

In other words, we learn something either way. Either we learn that the people we love are willing to respect our boundaries, or we learn that they are not willing. The data is valuable, even if it breaks our hearts.

The good news is, no matter how healthy or unhealthy our loved ones are at this moment, there is a safe way for us to achieve resolution with them. Even if it's not advisable or possible for these people to join us for a "real" conversation, we can still tell the truth and create healing for ourselves. We can still have closure anytime we want. (I share more about how this works in the no-owe invitation.)

On the deepest level, we're all connected, so we can talk to the essence of another person even if they're physically, mentally, and emotionally far away. If there is love in our hearts, we'll always be connected. And we can bring healing to the parts of ourselves that hurt, the parts of ourselves that love people who cannot currently love us well. Doing so is an act of service to ourselves and to all of humanity.

THE NO-OWE INVITATION

You Owe Yourself an Interaction

First, an important note: this is similar to the "Follow the Energy Back" exercise in that it's deep, emotional-level work. As such, you may wish to find a trained counselor to support you in this practice. It can bring up some difficult issues, and it's important that you have emotional support in place for when the big feelings rise. If after reading through the invitation you feel that you need additional support, please seek it out. I share these tools so that you have them accessible when you are prepared to dive deep. It's counterproductive to rush the process or push yourself past your emotional capacity.

This is an invitation to do an "imagined," Gestalt-based dialogue with someone you love and say how you really feel.

Find a quiet, protected time when you won't be interrupted. Go into a room with at least two places to sit, and close the door. As before, begin by centering yourself in your loving heart space and by setting your intention to heal. As you'll recall, this simply means getting still and connecting to an experience of love within yourself. It might be love for a child, partner, or pet; all that matters is that you activate a feeling of love flowing to and from you. Once you've done that, set a positive intention to heal. (The words I typically use are, "My intention is to heal at the deepest level possible.")

Once you've done that, pick someone, living or dead, with whom you have a challenging relationship. Imagine that that person has come to speak with you; imagine them entering the room where you are now. Wait until you can imagine or sense them sitting across from you. Then start talking.

Say everything you'd say if you were totally unafraid of their reaction. Tell the truth, the whole truth, and nothing but the truth. Tell them everything you feel and think about them. Let it take as long as it takes. When you feel complete, then switch chairs. Now speak to yourself as though you were the other person, answering all of those accusations, questions, angers, and confusions. Go back and forth, working to resolve the issues between you. Listen closely; you may be surprised by what you hear. If it feels hard, remember that you can pause or stop the dialogue at any time if you feel overwhelmed; you are the one in control here.

There may be times when you discover that the other person's energy is not willing to cooperate enough to have a constructive conversation. That's painful yet valuable information for you. In those cases, you can still come to a resolution within yourself. You can still get closure about the nature of the relationship or wish them well regardless of what they think of you.

For example, when I did an "empty chair" dialogue with someone from my past, the words "they" spoke were abusive. I was shaken at first, but then I was able to say, "I'm not available for that. I love you, and for so long that was all that mattered. But now I love me too, and I'm not willing to stay in this space with you when you speak to me that way. When you're ready to meet me with respect, I'm willing to talk again." "They" were not pleased with this and responded with more hurtful words. Though the other person wasn't physically there, it was a powerful practice for me to draw a line and step out of the dialogue. "Goodbye. I wish you well."

If you are struggling with this dialogue at any point, or if you simply sense that you would benefit from having additional support, invite your future self to join the conversation. Just as you imagined inviting the other person to join you, invite Future You to come into the room where you are. Imagine that Future You is already everything you have longed to be; picture her radiant, whole, and fully healed. (You can also refer to Future You as Authentic Wisdom, Spirit, or whatever name feels right to you.)

Imagine that Future You is eager to support you in your growth so that you can become her. Allow Future You to be your ally and advocate. Ask her questions, and listen closely to the wisdom that comes through Future You. You might be surprised!

When you're complete with the dialogue, thank the other person for coming to talk with you, and thank Future You for coming as well, if she supported you in this exercise. Once you've said goodbye, praise yourself for a job well done. After that, look at the projections, judgments, and limiting beliefs that arose in the dialogue, and offer yourself forgiveness for each one.

Epilogue

You Don't Owe Anyone, Period
(You Are Free)

The ultimate authority of my life is not the Bible; it is not confined between the covers of a book. It is not something written by men and frozen in time. It is not from a source outside myself. My ultimate authority is the divine voice in my own soul. Period.

—Sue Monk Kidd, *The Dance of the Dissident Daughter*

DID YOU KNOW THAT the mythological phoenix—the iconic bird who rises, reborn, from its own ashes—actually starts the fire as well? The phoenix isn't a victim; it chooses the flames of transformation. It destroys its own comfort zone. It sets both its nest and its old self ablaze.

Have you ever done that, metaphorically speaking? Have you ever burned down the old to make room for the new? Ever set your comfort zone on fire, on purpose? If you have, then you know that it's deeply uncomfortable. It burns.

The phoenix only chooses the pain of the fire when the pain of staying the same is greater.

If you want to make a positive change in your life but you're afraid of the pain it will take to do it, that's normal. But as you're weighing the fear, remember that you'll feel pain either way. I learned this powerful concept from coach Brooke Castillo. She says that approximately 50 percent of the time that you're awake, you're going to feel uncomfortable. Either you're in pain because you're renewing your life and growing your capacity, or you're in pain because you're constricting yourself and hiding from what's real.

It's discomfort either way. You just get to choose the type of pain you feel.

When you remind yourself that you don't owe anyone, you're acknowledging that your next move is always your choice. You can stay in your old nest, flinching against sharp bits of dry kindling. Or you can see what your world looks like lit up and aglow with fire.

Sometimes this transformation looks dramatic; sometimes you decide to change and your old life goes up in a big blaze very quickly. But more often it starts with small sparks in everyday moments. It's made manifest in how you greet your family members in the morning or how you choose to talk—or not talk—around the supper table at night.

"UNCLE RON, CAN YOU finish this for me?" My six-year-old niece wiped her face with her stars and stripes paper napkin and pointed to the last sauce-drenched pork barbecue rib on her Styrofoam plate. Twenty-five McGraw family members had gathered for this tremendous Fourth of July feast, and I knew that if Uncle Ron didn't eat that rib, someone else would.

I took another forkful of black-eyed peas, then sipped a little more ice water. Gazing out the window of Jonathan's family's Alabama lake house, I saw pontoon boats filled with families and WaveRunners revving up and down the sloughs. *Please, God, let this meal be over soon. I just can't deal with any more comments about me not eating the pork.*

"You bet, little lady!" Uncle Ron smiled. He took the meat and then—yes—actually swished it under my nose. "Mmm, smells good, doesn't it?"

Each year, he would smile and joke about the fact that I didn't eat the pork barbecue. Yet in the teasing words, I heard an undertone: *C'mon, stop being so stubborn. Just eat the ribs like the rest of us.*

"Mmm!" I hummed back with as much playfulness as I could muster. The McGraws had always been generous to me, and I wanted to be generous to them. But after a few days spent in close quarters with a dozen family members, this was getting harder and harder to do.

Jonathan and I had been married for nearly five years, and I was tired of repeating myself. I was tired of saying, as politely as possible, "I'm sure the pork is delicious. You enjoy it! When I was growing up, my church was strict about pork being off-limits, so I guess it's still in my head."

Most relatives nodded and dropped the subject. But some just couldn't let it go.

That evening, it was one barbecue rib too much for me. Desperate for a little space, I set off for a solo walk. The intense heat of the day was fading as I started out. Up the driveway, onto the main road, past the house with the yapping dogs, then to the little grove of scrub bushes where Jonathan and I watched dozens of fireflies blink in synchronized rhythms at night.

In a recent session, my counselor had challenged me to notice and question "should" statements in my thinking, and that night I had plenty of material. *Shouldn't you stay back with the others? Why do you need to go on this walk? And why do you need to eat differently? Shouldn't you be like everyone else? What's wrong with you?*

Wow, I thought, trying to simply observe the thought stream rather than attach to it. It took effort, but when I watched my thoughts, the reason for my distress became clearer. *No wonder I have trouble with lake vacations. The problem isn't Uncle Ron—or anyone else, for that matter. The problem is that I take other people's words and use them to be really mean to myself. It's me who is causing me to suffer here.*

The force of that realization brought me to my knees. Carefully, I sat back on my heels and stood up to the bully in my head. Finally, I answered her most insistent, burning question: *Why can't you just not be who you are?*

"Because I can't," I said out loud. "If I stopped being myself, I wouldn't be real."

For once in my life, it was exactly that simple.

The sky above me blazed, then traded the pinks and reds of sunset for the blues and purples of twilight. The residual heat from the asphalt seeped through my shorts and warmed my legs. I sat for ten minutes, or perhaps I sat forever. It was hard to say. I was simply present, surrendered and still, breathing in and breathing out.

On my way back to the lake house, I passed a neighboring pasture. A horse with a chestnut coat waited for me by the barbed-wire fence, as though we had some kind of cosmic appointment. When I reached him, he nuzzled my hand. Then one by one, three other horses joined us. All at once, it was Tam wrapping me in a blanket and Brooke handing me a glass of water. It was Raymond purring and Jonathan subbing in for me on morning routine at L'Arche. The Presence had arrived, and the Presence had always been there.

"Thank you. Good horse. Thank you," I repeated to the palomino who stood by me for a long time, watching me as I wept. In response, the palomino folded me into a horse hug and anointed me with kisses, gentle and smelly and entirely perfect.

A WEEK AFTER JONATHAN and I returned from the lake house, he was busy with home renovations, so I decided to do the obvious thing and blast Florence and the Machine for a solo dance party. When I turned on "Shake It Out," Florence Welch's distinctive voice rang out, and our cat Bootsie bolted. Music scared her, but it had to be done.

"Sorry, kitty cat," I said, with no regret whatsoever. "It's Tuesday night, and it's time to shake it out. Florence is a goddess."

Dancing around our living room holding an imaginary microphone, I careened around the sofa, chairs, and coffee table. I went from my old figure skating moves to dirty dancing and back. I did salchows and spirals; I rolled my hips and dropped it low.

I'd heard an interview with Florence in which she'd described the song's opening organ chords as "optimistic and sad at the same time," and that summed up exactly how I felt. Florence was singing about not being able to leave her past behind, but that was what the anthem—with its drums, bells, and gorgeous vocals—was helping me to do. I could leave the past behind not because it didn't matter, but because it was already present with me; it was folded into who I was and who I would become. For a little while, at least, I left behind all ideas of past, present, and future and just danced in the now.

Dancing brought me to that place that Rumi wrote about, the field beyond concepts of wrongdoing and rightdoing. It was a place with no separation between people. It was the heaven I'd dreamed about as a little girl, where I could ask my brother any question and receive a true answer. It was the awareness that Willie and our parents had their own stories, their own journeys, of which I was only a part. In the end, I didn't owe them, and they didn't owe me. Without thoughts of wrongdoing and rightdoing, only love for all of us remained.

There was drowning-deep sadness in this life, yes. But when I danced, I found that I could float on the dark water.

It was dark outside too, save for the flickering of one finicky streetlight. For a beat, I wondered if anyone could see me through the second-floor windows. Yet the thought of being visible didn't really bother me. As the music played, I didn't care about anything other than the wild energy coursing through my body.

Shimmying over to our built-in bookcase, I let my hands graze the spines of several beloved books before pausing over my old Bible. The volume had been with me ever since a youth missions conference in early 2006; I'd carried it through eight years and five moves. At the conference, we'd studied the book of Ephesians, so the front cover read, "Live a life worthy of the calling" in fancy calligraphic script. Still swaying my shoulders to the music, I held the book in my hands. It was soft with use and yellowed with age, its whisper-thin pages dingy around the edges.

It was by all appearances a well-used, well-loved Bible, but the truth was that I hadn't read it in two years. I'd pick it up sometimes, leafing through the pages in hopes of conjuring up the comfort I used to feel at the sight of familiar verses. But then authoritarian voices from my past would come shrieking out as though that Bible was one of those talking books in Harry Potter's world, and I'd shove the volume back onto the shelf. That night, with Florence and the Machine blaring around me, the book felt so heavy. It was a deadweight that I wanted gone, gone, gone. *What if I just tore it up into tiny pieces?* I thought.

Though I hesitated, I knew that desire to tear apart that old Bible wasn't about disrespect or dishonor. All I wanted was to let go of everything that had ever kept me from dancing.

THE NEXT DAY WAS a Wednesday, so our recycling bins needed to be brought to the curb that morning. With deliberation and caution, I headed back to the bookcase. I picked up the Bible once more and studied the front cover quote again. At age twenty-one, I heard "Live a life worthy of the calling you have received" as a rousing call to action. At twenty-nine, those same words filled me with shame and distress. My own faults and frailties loomed too large; I saw so many ways I'd failed to measure up to the perfect standard. But then I looked at the subsequent words, the smaller print: "Be completely humble and gentle; be patient, bearing with one another in love."

Reading that, I wondered what other small print I'd missed. Maybe a worthy life was never about being flawless. Maybe it was always about love and humility.

I thought of Theo, one of the core members I'd been close to at L'Arche. One evening when we were all gathered around the dinner table, Harley asked him, "What does it mean to be human?" And Theo responded, "To be humble."

At the time, I'd thought that was profound in itself. But Harley added another question. "OK, but what does it mean to be humble?"

"Well, I don't know," Theo replied. "But I think it helps . . . not to be afraid of your faults."

As I took another look at the peeling Bible cover, I thought about Theo's words. And I wondered if the person with whom I needed to be patient and gentle, to bear with in love, was myself.

In that spirit, I picked up the Bible and brought it to the curb along with our latest recyclables. The air was dense and muggy as I stepped out from the porch, upending the bag of recycling into the grimy green bin. The trees in our front yard formed a vibrant green canopy above my head; after the rains the day before, they were Crayola-crayon bright.

I gave the Bible one last squeeze and whispered, "Namaste"— *the light within me recognizes and honors the light within you*—before laying it gently to rest with the newspapers and the junk mail, the aluminum cans and the plastic containers.

Moving respectfully and calmly, I carried the bin to the curb, conducting a ceremony of my own making. I had a flicker of superstitious fear: *Will God throw a lightning bolt at me for this?* In my heart, though, I knew better. God had never punished me. Only I'd punished me. And little by little, I was learning how not to do that anymore.

As a child, I'd thought of heaven as a place without barriers, a place wherein I could ask my brother any question and receive a true, complete answer. No one had taught me that idea; it had arisen from within. Letting go of my old Bible was just another way of trusting that inner knowing. At the curb, I whispered a favorite verse from the Bible I'd just released: "The only thing that counts is faith expressing itself through love."

In that moment, I chose to believe that my faults and failures weren't what counted. I chose to believe that I didn't owe anyone. I chose to believe that I was free.

CHOOSING IN THIS WAY takes practice and patience; it takes time for us to build up our capacity for freedom. I'm still building mine, that's for sure. But here's what I've come to know: We can begin here, now, today. This moment is always the perfect time to start. Everything that has happened so far culminates right here.

We cannot know why it has happened this way, up until now. Why has there been so much damage, so much suffering? And why does it

continue? Personally, I cannot accept any pat answer or easy reassurance. I cannot believe anyone who tries to tie it all up in a neat bow
for me, glossing over grief and bypassing pain.

And yet, I can accept this much: If any of the turns my life has
taken had been different, where I am now would be different. If I had
missed any part of my path along the way, I would not be here, now,
writing these words to you. And I wouldn't have missed this journey
with you for the world.

As Byron Katie has said, "We just can't know more than God. We
can't know what is best for our path; all I can know about my path is
I've had the perfect one for me."

That's one road to freedom: The realization that we've had the perfect path *for ourselves*. Not for anyone else. No one's story is quite like
ours. So how could we ever pass judgment when it's all still unfolding?

A FEW HOURS AFTER I recycled my Bible, I returned from the
library to find the recycling bin empty. My old comfort and albatross
was gone. With a swing in my step, I checked the mailbox. Would my
check from that new client come in today? It was due by the fifteenth,
and today was . . .

Turning my sports watch, I registered the digital readout: July 16,
2014. "Oh. My. God." I said aloud. Unbeknownst to my conscious mind
at least, I'd recycled my Bible on the fourteenth anniversary of my
baptism.

It wasn't an ending at all. It was just one more chance to light
the old nest on fire and see what rose from the ashes. It was just one
more opportunity to trust what my own heart promised me: *Honey, it
will be beautiful.*

THE NO-OWE INVITATION

Dance It Out ... Yes, Literally

Pick a time when you're alone and put on the song that gives you chills and makes you feel fully alive. Crank up the volume and move your body in whatever way feels best to you. Just for this moment, give up everything that feels heavy and confining. Embrace a spirituality of lightness, grace, and freedom. Let yourself go. Let yourself be moved. Let it happen.

I don't owe anyone. You don't owe anyone. That's what grace means.

Acknowledgments

I'VE ALWAYS LOVED THE line from Meister Eckhart: "If the only prayer you ever say in your entire life is thank you, it will be enough." In that spirit, thank you to everyone who appears in these pages. I'm grateful for everything you have taught me.

Thank you to all of the readers at A Wish Come Clear. It is an honor to write to you and for you. (I'm wildly biased, but I think our little corner of the internet is particularly special.)

Thank you to my private coaching clients; it's a joy to support you on your journeys.

Thank you to my agent Angela Scheff for helping this book find a home and hanging in there for the whole wild ride. I'm so lucky to work with a kindred spirit like you. Thank you to the team at the Christopher Ferebee Agency for all the work you do.

Thank you to my editor Lil Copan for taking a chance on me and this manuscript. Your edits were invaluable, and I'm grateful for you and the rest of the team at Broadleaf Books.

Thank you to Addie Zierman for reading and editing an early draft of this book, back when it was still a memoir. You helped me tremendously. (And the Christy Miller notepad—priceless.)

Thank you to Rob Bell for telling me that I was more rebellious than I realized and that my book was more subversive than I thought. (You were right.)

Thank you to my husband, Jonathan, for everything you've done to help me make this dream of authorship a reality (including the brilliant book title). With you, I can see that it really is "all just gift." That said, I don't know how I can face the future when I know there are eight quarts of these pickles in it—but for you, anything. I love you today and always.

Thank you to our little one(s), simply for being. I love you so. The way that you are is a wonderful way.

Thank you to Brooke: This book is much better because of you, as is my life in general. You're my person, OK? Don't make a big deal about it. Whatever. Love, love, and love again. (And also, what a *result*!)

Thank you to Tam: Honey bunches! Thank you for sharing every adventure of this ordinary, extraordinary life with me. (*About Time* reference, obviously.) You are the storm and the silver lining. I love you a million red M&Ms.

Thank you to Dad, Mom, and Willie, and the extended Fischer, Maline, and McGraw families, for your love and generous support.

Thank you to the SEP UK community, the Vassar College community, the L'Arche GWDC community, everyone at The Clearing (especially Joe Koelzer and Betsy Koelzer, Scott Alpert, and our August 2016 cohort), and the kindred spirits here in our Alabama town.

Notes & Works Cited

With gratitude, the author acknowledges the following artists:

Introduction

Pullman, Philip. Quote via Goodreads. Accessed July 31, 2020. https://tinyurl.com/y4drpsx7.

1 *You Don't Owe Anyone* the Good Child

Anonymous. "The Dangers of the Good Child." The School of Life. Accessed January 30, 2020. https://tinyurl.com/y4vrqlqy.

Lamott, Anne. *Bird by Bird.* New York: Anchor, 1995.

Oliver, Mary. *Dream Work.* Boston: Atlantic Monthly Press, 1986.

Opposite-hand writing exercise learned at The Clearing in August 2016. Curriculum created by Joe Koelzer, Betsy Koelzer, and Scott Alpert based on the spiritual psychology curriculum of H. Ronald Hulnick and Mary R. Hulnick at the University of Santa Monica. The Clearing's inpatient dual diagnosis addiction treatment center is located at 2687 West Valley Road, Friday Harbor, WA 98250. Visit https://www.theclearingnw.com for more information.

2 *You Don't Owe Anyone* Your Spiritual Allegiance

Winterson, Jeanette. *Why Be Happy When You Could Be Normal?* New York: Grove Press, 2013.

Isaiah 11:6, paraphrase.

Baring-Gould, Sabine. "Onward Christian Soldiers." Music by Arthur Sullivan. Lyrics to "Onward Christian Soldiers" via herbert-w-armstrong .com. Accessed January 30, 2020. https://tinyurl.com/y3wfsbfw.

North, Katherine. *Holy Heathen*. Portland: Declare Dominion, 2020.

Grace Communion International. Wikipedia. Accessed July 31, 2020. https://tinyurl.com/y7cxfrob.

Armstrong, Herbert W. *The Plain Truth about Christmas*. Pasadena: Ambassador College, 1974. Archived on hwalibrary.com. Accessed January 30, 2020. https://tinyurl.com/yxz4a2t9.

Beck, Martha. *Leaving the Saints*. New York: Broadway Books, 2006.

Maté, Gabor. *When the Body Says No*. Hoboken: Wiley, 2011.

Lamott, Anne. *Blue Shoe*. New York: Riverhead Books, 2003.

Mark 14:6–8.

Cameron, Julia. *The Artist's Way*. New York: Tarcher, 1992.

3   *You Don't Owe Anyone* a Savior

Lamott, Anne. "There's a whole chapter on perfectionism in *Bird by Bird*." Facebook, May 12, 2014. https://tinyurl.com/y4ubxxfc.

"Theory." The Bowen Center for the Study of the Family. Accessed July 31, 2020. https://thebowencenter.org/theory/.

"Dysfunctional Family Roles." Out of the Storm. Accessed July 31, 2020. https://tinyurl.com/y2xqsrab.

1 Corinthians 7:14.

Rein, Valerie. *Patriarchy Stress Disorder*. Austin: Lioncrest, 2019.

Winterson. *Why Be Happy*.

Video sermon by Tkach to Worldwide Church of God Members, January 1995. Transcribed at exitsupportnetwork.com. Accessed January 30, 2020. https://tinyurl.com/y484xa68.

Green, John. *The Fault in Our Stars*. New York: Penguin, 2014.

Katie, Byron. "Enlightened Activism." The Work of Byron Katie. Accessed July 31, 2020. https://tinyurl.com/yyjwgctr.

Projections exercise learned at The Clearing in August 2016. Curriculum created by Joe Koelzer, Betsy Koelzer, and Scott Alpert based on the spiritual psychology curriculum of H. Ronald Hulnick and

Mary R. Hulnick at the University of Santa Monica. The Clearing's inpatient dual diagnosis addiction treatment center is located at 2687 West Valley Road, Friday Harbor, WA 98250. Visit https://www .theclearingnw.com/ for more information.

4 *You Don't Owe Anyone* a Brave Face

Corner, Lewis. "I Thought I Would Be Dead by Now." Interview with Natalia Kills. Digital Spy. Accessed August 4, 2020. https://tinyurl .com/y3bovyyy.
2 Corinthians 12:10.
Picoult, Jody. *My Sister's Keeper*. New York: Atria, 2004.
Cambridge English Dictionary. S.v. "Brave." Accessed August 5, 2020. https://tinyurl.com/yxjdcru3.
Doyle, Glennon. *Untamed*. New York: Dial Press, 2020.
Beck, Martha. *The Joy Diet*. New York: Harmony, 2003.
Lamott, Anne. *Bird by Bird*. New York: Anchor Books, 1995.
Katie, Byron. "The Work." The Work of Byron Katie. Accessed January 30, 2020. https://tinyurl.com/y3uyyluf.

5 *You Don't Owe Anyone* Your Forgiveness

Gilbert, Elizabeth. "FORGIVENESS, continued." Facebook, December 17, 2014. https://tinyurl.com/y5333ajt.
Beck, Martha. *The Joy Diet*. New York: Harmony, 2003.
Barton, Julie. *Dog Medicine*. New York: Penguin, 2016.
Beck, Martha. "Taking the Weight Off . . . Again." *O, The Oprah Magazine*, January 2007. Accessed August 10, 2020. https://tinyurl.com/y2apq3zk.
Nani, Christel. *Diary of a Medical Intuitive*. Cayucos: L. M. Press, 2004.
Horton, Peter, dir. *Grey's Anatomy*. Season 2, episode 1, "Raindrops Keep Falling on My Head." Written by Stacy McKee. Aired September 25, 2005, on ABC.
Self-forgiveness exercise learned at The Clearing in August 2016. Curriculum created by Joe Koelzer, Betsy Koelzer, and Scott Alpert based

on the spiritual psychology curriculum of H. Ronald Hulnick and
Mary R. Hulnick at the University of Santa Monica. The Clearing's
inpatient dual diagnosis addiction treatment center is located at
2687 West Valley Road, Friday Harbor, WA 98250. Visit https://www
.theclearingnw.com/ for more information.

6 You Don't Owe Anyone Superhuman Strength

Nepo, Mark. *The Book of Awakening*. Newburyport: Red Wheel, 2000.
Exodus 20:8.
L'Engle, Madeleine. *A Circle of Quiet*. New York: HarperOne, 1984.
Goldman, William. *The Princess Bride*. New York: Harcourt, 2007.
Havrilesky, Heather. "Ask Polly: Is He in Love with Me, or Has He Broken
   Me?" The Cut, October 12, 2016. Accessed August 18, 2020. https://
   tinyurl.com/y297rnkg.
Paul, Margaret. *Inner Bonding*. New York: HarperOne, 1992.
Awosika, Ayodeji. *Real Help*. Kindle edition. Independently published,
   December 2019.
Walker, Pete. *The Tao of Fully Feeling*. Berkeley: Azure Coyote, 2015.
Stern, Robin. *The Gaslight Effect*. New York: Harmony, 2007.
Spinazzola, Joseph. "Childhood Psychological Abuse as Harmful as Sex-
   ual or Physical Abuse." American Psychological Association, Octo-
   ber 8, 2014. Accessed August 18, 2020. https://tinyurl.com/y3dynhb4.
Beck, Martha. "Escape Your Rat Race." *O, The Oprah Magazine*, January
   2009. Accessed January 30, 2020. https://tinyurl.com/y3q7o65y.

7 You Don't Owe Anyone Your Compliance

Firman, John, and Ann Gila. *The Primal Wound*. Albany: State University
   of New York Press, 1997.
Sivers, Derek. "No 'Yes.' Either 'HELL YEAH!' or 'No.'" Sivers.org,
   August 26, 2009. Accessed January 30, 2020. https://sivers.org/hellyeah.
Cloud, Henry, and John Townsend. *Boundaries*. Revised edition. Grand
   Rapids: Zondervan, 1992.

Brown, Brené. *Rising Strong*. Reprint edition. New York: Random House, 2017.

Gilbert, Elizabeth. "THE ALPHA MARE." Facebook, June 21, 2016. https://tinyurl.com/y4jbqtsj.

Grant, Adam. *Give and Take*. Reprint edition. New York: Penguin Books, 2014.

Encyclopedia Britannica Online. S.v. "Gestalt psychology." Accessed August 18, 2020. https://tinyurl.com/y6f5jdlp.

Follow the energy back exercise learned at The Clearing in August 2016. Curriculum created by Joe Koelzer, Betsy Koelzer, and Scott Alpert based on the spiritual psychology curriculum of H. Ronald Hulnick and Mary R. Hulnick at the University of Santa Monica. The Clearing's inpatient dual diagnosis addiction treatment center is located at 2687 West Valley Road, Friday Harbor, WA 98250. Visit https://www.theclearingnw.com/ for more information.

8 *You Don't Owe Anyone* an Explanation

Doyle, Glennon. "I Support Your Right to Share My Rights." Huffpost.com, April 7, 2015. Accessed December 17, 2020. https://tinyurl.com/y57jkeup.

Beck, Martha. "Impotent Rage: Why Are You So Angry Inside?" Oprah.com, October 2004. Accessed August 26, 2020. https://tinyurl.com/yybojdr9.

Matthew 10:29–31.

Rohr, Richard. *Radical Grace: Daily Meditations*. Cincinnati: St. Anthony Messenger Press, 1995.

Smirnova, Daria, et al. "Language Patterns Discriminate Mild Depression from Normal Sadness and Euthymic State." *Frontiers in Psychiatry* 9, no. 105 (April 10, 2018). https://doi.org/10.3389/fpsyt.2018.00105.

Jobs, Steve. "'You've Got to Find What You Love,' Jobs Says." Stanford News, June 14, 2005. Accessed August 25, 2020. https://news.stanford.edu/2005/06/14/jobs-061505/.

Brontë, Charlotte. *Jane Eyre*. Reprint edition. New York: Penguin Classics, 2006.

9 *You Don't Owe Anyone* Your Time and Energy

Strayed, Cheryl. *Tiny Beautiful Things*. New York: Vintage, 2012.

Havrilesky, Heather. "Ask Polly: I Work Too Hard and I'm Still Poor and Miserable!" The Cut, October 11, 2017. Accessed August 18, 2020. https://tinyurl.com/y3eur9lx.

TMF Project (@tmfproject). "What do you want to do? That's the only question you need to answer." Twitter, March 1, 2001, 6:42 a.m. https://tinyurl.com/y3pkjhh3.

Beck, Martha. *The Joy Diet*. New York: Harmony, 2003.

Ben-Shahar, Tal. "4 Ways to Create Small Moments of Happiness In Your Life." Thrive Global, February 10, 2019. Accessed December 29, 2020. https://tinyurl.com/ydyzg27v.

Modified version of the ideal scene / affirmation exercises originally learned at The Clearing in August 2016. Curriculum created by Joe Koelzer, Betsy Koelzer, and Scott Alpert based on the spiritual psychology curriculum of H. Ronald Hulnick and Mary R. Hulnick at the University of Santa Monica. The Clearing's inpatient dual diagnosis addiction treatment center is located at 2687 West Valley Road, Friday Harbor, WA 98250. Visit https://www.theclearingnw.com/ for more information.

10 *You Don't Owe Anyone* an Interaction

Westover, Tara. *Educated*. New York: Random House, 2018.

Mark 8:36.

"We Are the Committee." October 29, 2017. *The RobCast from Rob Bell*. Podcast. https://tinyurl.com/y5twxr65.

Psalm 19:1–2.

Hendricks, Gay. *The Big Leap*. New York: HarperOne, 2010.

Redwine, Andie, dir. *Paradise Recovered*. 2010; La Vergne, TN: Monarch Video, 2012. DVD.

Beck, Martha. "The New You: Handling Change-Back Attacks." MarthaBeck.com, October 2012. Accessed August 26, 2020. https://tinyurl.com/yxbn63wt.

Paul, Margaret. *Inner Bonding.* New York: HarperOne, 1992.

Gestalt exercise first learned at The Clearing in August 2016. Curriculum created by Joe Koelzer, Betsy Koelzer, and Scott Alpert based on the spiritual psychology curriculum of H. Ronald Hulnick and Mary R. Hulnick at the University of Santa Monica. The Clearing's inpatient dual diagnosis addiction treatment center is located at 2687 West Valley Road, Friday Harbor, WA 98250. Visit https://www.theclearingnw.com/ for more information.

Epilogue

Kidd, Sue Monk. *The Dance of the Dissident Daughter.* Revised edition. New York: HarperOne, 2016.

Castillo, Brooke. "Discomfort on Purpose." June 28, 2018. *The Life Coach School.* Podcast. https://thelifecoachschool.com/podcast/222/.

Montgomery, James. "Florence and the Machine Get 'Satanic' in 'Shake It Out' Video." MTV News, October 26, 2011. Accessed October 27, 2011, https://tinyurl.com/y62d25qz.

Rumi (Jalāl ad-Dīn Muhammad Rūmī). "Out beyond Ideas." National Poetry Day. Accessed August 26, 2020. https://tinyurl.com/yxdha7qv.

Ephesians 4:1–2.

Galatians 5:6.

Katie, Byron. *Who Would You Be without Your Story?* Carlsbad: Hay House, 2008.

Acknowledgments

Eckhart, Meister. Quote via Goodreads. Accessed October 8, 2020. https://tinyurl.com/y3otspz9.